# CHILDREN
## of the
## U.S.A.

# CHILDREN of the U.S.A.

Maya Ajmera

Yvonne Wakim Dennis

Arlene Hirschfelder

Cynthia Pon

A GLOBAL FUND FOR
Children
BOOK

Charlesbridge

# CONTENTS

The chapters in this book feature fifty-one communities.

Come meet your peers from the city, the country, and the places in between!

# CONTENTS

# What is it like to be a child in

The children of the U.S.A. are light and dark and every shade in between. They are quiet and talkative, rich and poor, artistic and athletic and studious. They may be new immigrants just starting to discover this intriguing land, or their ancestors may have lived here for generations.

There is no typical American child. Each has his or her own history and heritage. For centuries people have been coming here from all over the world. Today kids share their customs, foods, and interests with kids from many other backgrounds. Together they eat hot dogs and tacos, play baseball and do karate, hip-hop and jam. They also discover the many things they have in common as they start to shape the future of this country.

*Children of the U.S.A.* celebrates the country's diversity. Featuring fifty-one U.S. towns and cities—one from each state, plus Washington, D.C., our nation's capital—this book presents aspects of more than one hundred cultural, ethnic, or religious groups. Across fields and on playgrounds, in high-rises and by the shore, it gives a glimpse of what life is like for kids living in the ever-changing mix that makes up the United States.

"My city is part of history, and I think that is very cool."

—Joey, age 9
Issaquah, Washington

"I like eating foods from different people. It makes eating less boring. Ithaca has everything from curries to Arabic food."

—Keenan, age 9
Trumansburg, New York

# the United States of America?

*Children of the U.S.A.* also shares some of the history that has formed the identity of each city and the nation as a whole. The United States is a country of immigrants: other than Native peoples, everyone here is from, or descended from people who came from, somewhere else. In the early days of this country, Native peoples saw their nations and lifeways torn apart and their lands taken by new immigrants. Today American Indians continue to honor their cultures, and their democratic beliefs and knowledge of agricultural science still shape American life. Many African Americans endured our nation's shameful history of slavery and racial inequality even as they helped build the foundation of this country. For more than four hundred years, Asian Americans have planted and built significant contributions to the nation, even though many were denied citizenship until the mid-twentieth century. Today recent African immigrants from Nigeria or Kenya teach in universities or own businesses next to those run by Asian newcomers from China, India, or Thailand.

> "Diversity means, to me, all kinds of people coming and forming a community."
>
> —Yazmin, age 9
> Clarksdale, Mississippi

> "My friends from different cultures have taught me that no matter your religion, color, ideas, or background, you can still be friends."
>
> —Corrie, age 12
> Raleigh, North Carolina

Like many immigrants, Latino Americans, with roots in countries such as Mexico and Peru, bring with them cultures and customs that are being woven into the fabric of the United States. Millions of American families can trace their origins to European countries from Scotland to Italy to Bulgaria. Others have ties to Middle Eastern countries like Israel and Lebanon. People have taken great risks to leave their home countries and journey to the United States, inspired by the promise of freedom and opportunity. Many encountered poverty, prejudice, and the challenge of learning a new language, but eventually began to leave their own important marks on the character of the nation.

In many cities today, children gather with their families on holy days at Jewish synagogues that stand right next to Christian churches, or Islamic mosques that sit across the street from Hindu temples. The freedom to practice any religion—or no religion—is a civil right of all Americans. Broad religious, ethnic, and cultural diversity is the backbone of American society, where children of a wide range of talents and physical and mental abilities have the right and opportunity to thrive.

Across the United States ideas and peoples mingle. The country is not perfect, and sometimes terrible mistakes are made. But the people of this land are creative and resilient. They learn from each other as they discover the many things they have in common, and they come to appreciate the things that make them different. The children of the U.S.A. are connected to children around the globe through family heritage, cultural traditions, and the hope for a fair, peaceful future. The tolerance and respect they learn from their own country's diversity may be the best gift they can share with the world.

"My friend is African American and she likes me a lot! I taught her an Arabic word and she taught me how to braid her hair."

—Sabrine, age 9
Dearborn, Michigan

"I have learned about my friends' cultures, and about the different parts of the world they are from. I have broadened my perspective on everyday things like food. I used to be unable to imagine meals without rice!"

—Jessica, age 13
Rockville, Maryland

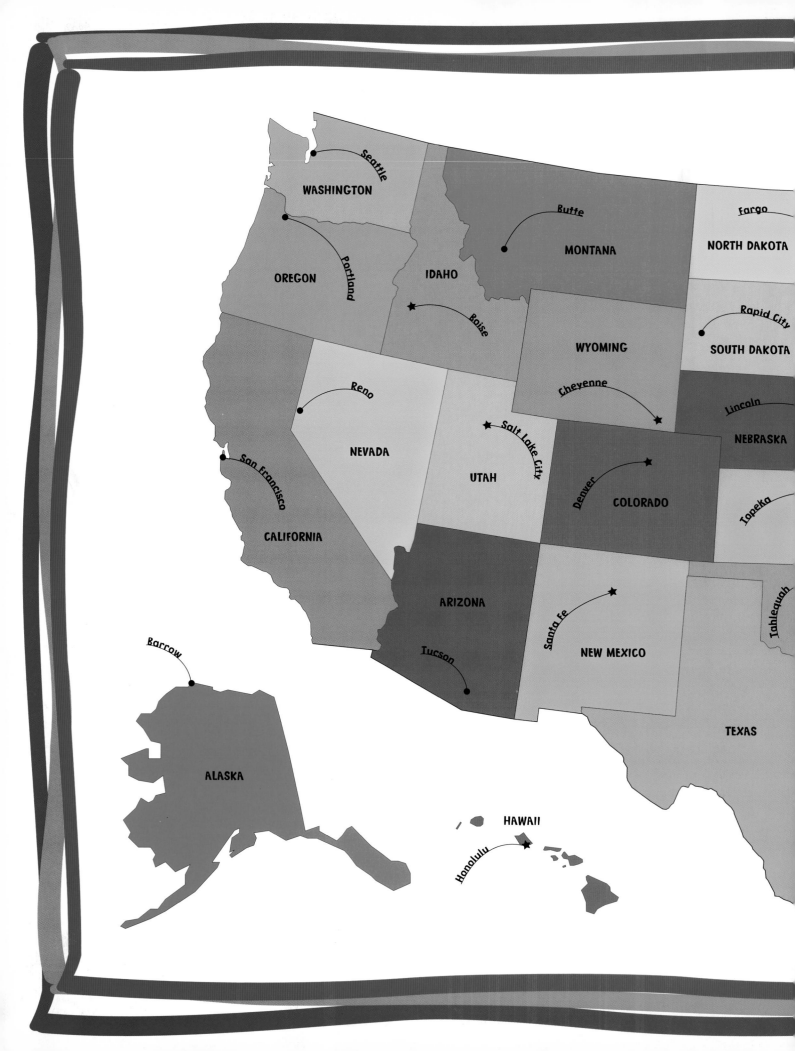

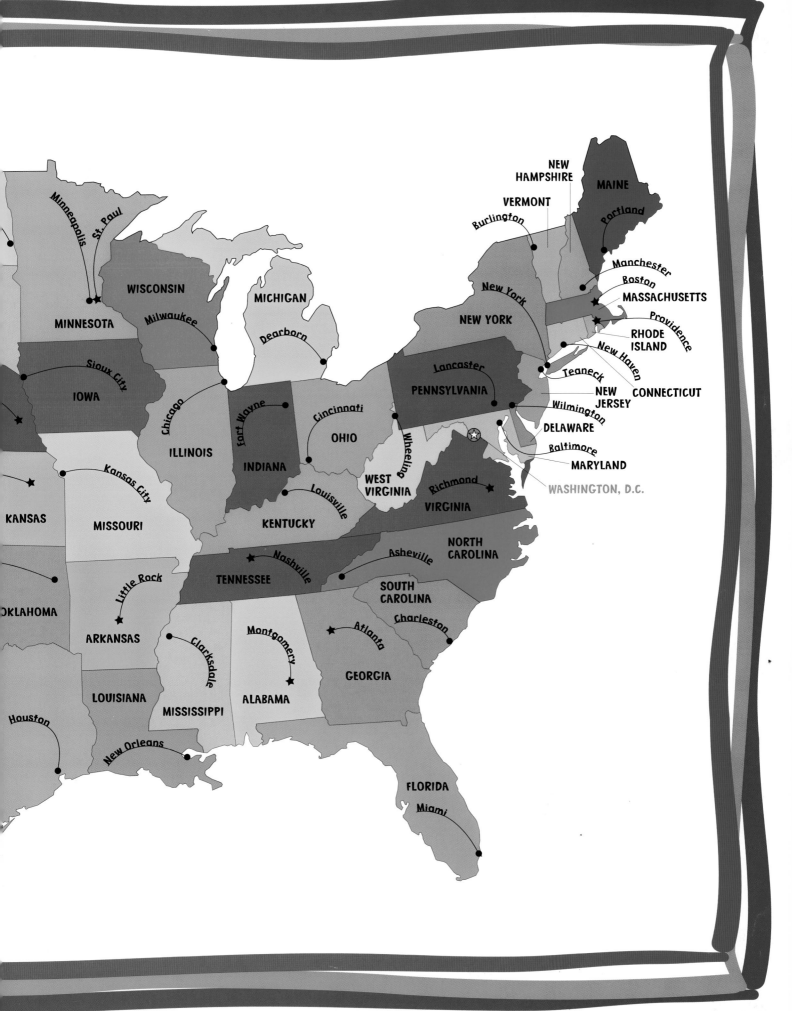

# MONTGOMERY

A first catch on Lake Martin!

Have you ever been asked to dinner without knowing who invited you? In 1983, during a period of tense race relations, thirty-five people in Montgomery received anonymous invitations to supper. At the restaurant, they met other guests from different cultures and backgrounds. Today members of the Friendly Supper Club still meet once a month to eat and talk about ordinary subjects like football, vacations, and car troubles. Their conversations help them understand each other's points of view and discover the many things they have in common.

Racial tensions were not new to Montgomery in the 1980s. Until the late 1950s and 1960s, legal segregation meant that African American kids in Montgomery and many other U.S. cities were not allowed to drink from the same public water fountains as white children, splash with them in public swimming pools, or ride side by side with them on city buses.

But Montgomery is also a place where ordinary citizens helped bring about social justice. On December 1, 1955, Rosa Parks, an African American woman and respected community leader, took a bus home as usual. The bus got crowded, and the driver demanded she give her seat to a white man and move to the back of the bus. When Parks refused to budge, the driver had her arrested. Clifford Durr, a white civil rights activist and attorney and Parks's longtime friend, bailed her out of jail.

The morning after Parks's arrest, Montgomery's black community launched a bus boycott. They asked a young Baptist minister named Martin Luther King, Jr., to lead the effort. The boycott began on December 5. For 381 days African

Celebrating a Flag Day parade with stars and stripes

14

Students design and build
a robot from scratch

Americans young and old refused to ride the city's buses. Instead they walked, rode bikes, or shared rides. The boycott succeeded. By the end of 1956, all people could ride Montgomery buses as equals. Eventually segregation of public facilities ended in other U.S. cities as well. Today downtown Montgomery is home to a civil rights memorial that honors the achievements of forty courageous people, including Dr. King, who gave their lives working for social justice.

Visiting Montgomery's Civil Rights Memorial

## More about
# Montgomery

**Founded:** 1819

**Total population:** 201,568

**Youth population:** 59,365

**Some languages heard in Montgomery:** Chinese, Greek, Igbo, Korean, Spanish

**Sister city:** None

15

# BARROW

A bear hug helps keep these kids warm

Snug in a traditional Iñupiaq parka

"Danger! Polar Bears!" The "Welcome to Barrow, Alaska" sign reminds visitors that Barrow is right in polar bear territory. The town garbage dump is located well outside the city so the bears will stop there instead of wandering into town for a meal.

Barrow, the northernmost city in the United States, is sometimes called the Top of the World. Because it is so close to the North Pole, it has twenty-four hours of daylight between May and August. Winter is a different story. The sun never rises between November and January. During the winter, the aurora borealis paints the sky with dancing colors. People come from around the world to see these spectacular northern lights.

Most Barrow residents are Iñupiat people whose ancestors have been living in the area for centuries. But people from Korea, the Philippines, the Balkan States, and Samoa also call Barrow home. Kids sing "Happy Birthday to You" in eleven languages at the only elementary school in town, the largest in Alaska. They also learn that there are more than thirty words for snow and ice in the Iñupiaq language!

Some Barrow students are talented moviemakers. The town's fourth graders produced the award-winning digital movie *Kivgiq*. Kivgiq is an Iñupiaq festival that features footraces, gift giving, and food made with caribou and seal meat. The festival draws indigenous dance groups from Russia, Canada, and Greenland.

At the Iñupiat Heritage Center, elders and artists teach kids the skills they need to live in a place that is often sixty degrees below zero. Young athletes develop physical strength for Arctic survival by learning games like the knuckle hop and ear pull. Many train all year to participate in the World Eskimo-Indian Olympics.

In the springtime melting snow means big puddles

Although people travel in cars around town, the only way in and out of Barrow is by plane or ship. Indigenous people from this part of the world invented the dogsled for transportation. Dogsledding is still part of Barrow, although today kids are more likely to get around town by snowmobile. After a day of snowmobiling or other outdoor sports, they can enjoy burritos and tacos at Pepe's North of the Border, the northernmost Mexican restaurant in the world.

Learning computer skills at the Top of the World

## More about
# Barrow

**Founded:** around 500

**Total population:** 4,581

**Youth population:** 1,822

**Nickname:** Top of the World

**Some languages heard in Barrow:** Iñupiaq, Macedonian, Samoan, Spanish, Tagalog

**Sister cities:** Inuvik, Canada; Ushuaia, Argentina

17

# TUCSON

Proud of his *paakiw,* or "fish" in the Hopi language

At the O'odham Tash parade

If you like to dance to hip-hop, sing opera, play the drums, paint murals, or write poetry, Tucson (TOO-sawn) is the city for you! Tucson kids have tons of opportunities to pursue arts from many cultures. Tucson, one of the oldest cities in the United States, has been a crossroads of cultures for centuries. A blend of American Indians, Mexicans, Asians, and Anglos live in the area and practice their arts. Recently Bantus from Somalia, in eastern Africa, have expanded the rich cultural mix.

About one-third of Tucson's population hails from Mexico, sixty miles to the south. Mexican mariachi music is wildly popular in Tucson. Musicians play and sing in restaurants or stroll the streets, dressed in studded *charro* (Mexican cowboy) outfits with wide-brimmed hats. Teenagers learn popular songs about love, death, and politics. Kids can also learn to play violins, guitars, and trumpets mariachi-style.

Starting in the 1970s Tucson's Mexican American artists began painting huge, colorful murals on the sides of white adobe buildings. The murals, which are not meant to be permanent, are often painted over with new scenes. In 1996 artists from the Tucson Arts Brigade invited kids and elders to work together to design and create murals in city neighborhoods. The bold and colorful acrylic brushstrokes recount important events or tell stories that are just plain fun.

Today's Tohono O'odham people are descended from the first Tucsonans. Over the years the Tohono O'odhams borrowed from cultures around them to create the *waila* (WHY-la) polka. *Waila* comes from *baile*, the Spanish word for "dance." This centuries-old folk music combines traditional Tohono O'odham tunes with fiddles introduced by Spanish missionaries and accordions brought by German immigrants. *Waila* polka bands also include drums, guitars, and saxophones. Dancers glide smoothly instead of hopping quickly as European polka dancers do. The blazing sun and heat in the Sonoran Desert make it too hot to move very fast! At *waila* festivals, kids from all over Tucson join in the fun.

All smiles in a Latina frock with ruffles of *azul* (blue) *y amarillo* (and yellow)

Painting a mural with the Tucson Arts Brigade

## More about
# Tucson

**Founded:** 1775

**Total population:** 486,699

**Youth population:** 139,499

**Nickname:** Old Pueblo

**Some languages heard in Tucson:** Arabic, Chinese, O'odham, Somali, Spanish

**Sister cities:** Almaty, Kazakhstan; Segovia, Spain

ARIZONA

# LITTLE ROCK

Admiring the famous Peabody ducks

Double the fun at the state fair

There actually is a "little rock" in Little Rock, the capital of Arkansas. The city was named for a stone bluff on the south bank of the Arkansas River. However, most of the rock was blown up in the late 1800s during the construction of a railroad bridge. From the city's Riverfront Park, you can see what's left of this landmark.

Little Rock was the setting for an important struggle for civil rights. In 1954 the U.S. Supreme Court declared that segregation of public schools was illegal. In 1957 six African American girls and three African American boys enrolled in Little Rock's all-white Central High School. The governor called in the state National Guard to prevent the nine students from entering the school. President Dwight Eisenhower responded by sending U.S. Army troops to escort them safely to class.

That didn't end the troubles! Many students hissed and threw things at their new classmates. But other students accepted the newcomers, making friends with them and helping them with their homework. The nine students never gave up going to school, even though some hostility continued. In 1999 President Bill Clinton, an Arkansan, honored the Little Rock Nine with Congressional Gold Medals for selfless heroism. Today Central High is racially diverse, and many of its students go to the nation's best colleges. The building has been named a National Historic Landmark because one of the most important events in U.S. history happened there.

Blacks now make up forty percent of Little Rock's population. They live, work, play, and attend school in a city far different from Little Rock in the 1950s. A growing population of Spanish-speaking people also call the city home. They come mainly from Mexico, California, and Texas. A handful of *mercados*

Celebrating Cinco de Mayo

(Mexican markets) have popped up in Little Rock. Now shoppers can easily find *nopalitos* (tender cactus) and jalapeño peppers. Little Rockans can also sample mouthwatering Greek pastries made with phyllo dough, butter, nuts, and spices at the annual Greek Food Festival. Little Rock's increasing cultural diversity livens up this river-port city.

Enjoying a favorite story with a friend

**ARKANSAS**

## More about
## Little Rock

**Founded:** 1831

**Total population:** 183,133

**Youth population:** 49,935

**Nickname:** City of Roses

**Some languages heard in Little Rock:** Greek, Japanese, Russian, Spanish, Tagalog

**Sister cities:** Changchun, China; Mons, Belgium

21

# SAN FRANCISCO

Parading a vibrant dragon in Chinatown

Going for the gold!

San Francisco has always been a multicultural town. Its mild climate, Pacific coastline, and majestic views have attracted people for centuries. About forty different American Indian groups, each with its own territory, customs, and language, were the first to live in the coastal area around San Francisco. Life for American Indians changed after the Spanish sailed into San Francisco Bay in the late 1700s. Spanish priests founded Mission Dolores, one of California's twenty-one missions created to convert American Indians to Christianity. Although many American Indians died at the mission, a small population survived and became part of an American Indian community that still lives in the Bay Area.

In 1848 gold was discovered in California. Soon immigrants poured into San Francisco, headed for California's gold fields. In these early days, San Francisco was a town of shacks, tents, and rotting ships. Signs sprang up in Chinese, English, French, Spanish, and German. So many people came so fast that San Francisco became an instant city. Its population jumped from eight hundred people in 1848 to over twenty-five thousand in 1850!

Thousands of Chinese first came to California to pan for gold and to find work, mostly in railroad building. Today San Francisco has one of the largest Chinese communities in the Western Hemisphere. In Chinatown, shop signs are written in Chinese characters and dragons encircle lampposts. Chinese New Year is celebrated in January or February, depending on the cycle of the moon. Gorgeous floats, stilt walkers, and Chinese acrobats parade through the streets. A team of over one hundred men and women carry the Gum Lung (Golden Dragon). The dragon dances along, accompanied by six hundred thousand firecrackers to scare away evil spirits and bring good fortune.

A Shaky Town dad and daughter

Chinatown spills into North Beach, an area called the Little Italy of the West Coast. At one time thousands of Italians lived in the neighborhood. You can sense its Italian roots if you step into Saints Peter and Paul Church, where baseball great Joe DiMaggio got married, watch a bocce tournament, or follow your nose through garlicky pasta sauces to sweet, airy pastries. Proudly and deliciously, San Francisco celebrates its long tradition as a multicultural town.

Enjoying nature in urban San Francisco

## More about
# San Francisco

**Founded:** 1850

**Total population:** 776,733

**Youth population:** 127,344

**Nicknames:** Golden Gate City, Shaky Town

**Some languages heard in San Francisco:** Arabic, Chinese, Italian, Japanese, Spanish

**Sister cities:** Shanghai, China; Sydney, Australia

# DENVER

Dressed for a Native American powwow, a dancer patiently waits for his prize

Grasslands and gold. That's what brought people to the area now called Denver. The state capital, Denver is nicknamed the "Mile-High City" because it sits one mile above sea level on the high Colorado Plateau. Buffalo once grazed here, surrounded by a sea of grass. Cheyenne, Arapaho, and other American Indian hunters hunted these enormous animals.

In the late 1850s, the U.S. government began forcing American Indian nations onto reservations, taking their lands for new settlers and immigrants. But the indigenous peoples didn't disappear. Today many national American Indian organizations are headquartered in Denver.

In 1858 flakes of gold were discovered in creeks near present-day Denver. Thousands of miners charged to the area. They quickly established three mining towns that grew and merged into the city of Denver. After the gold supply fizzled, many gold seekers settled in the area permanently. Spanish settlers introduced long-horned cattle to the vast grasslands. They hired vaqueros (skilled cowboys from Spain and later from Mexico) to round up cattle and drive them to market. Today about a third of the city's people trace their roots to Mexico or to one of seventeen other Latin American countries.

After the Civil War, former slaves moved to the area to work on cattle ranches. More than a third of the cowboys in the West were African American. Many settled in Denver after they quit herding. Others worked on trains as railroad porters and settled in the neighborhoods around the end of the railroad line.

Making tracks with some help from a four-legged friend

Cooling off in the City Park fountain

Immigrants still come to the Mile-High City with high hopes for a better life. Eritreans, from Africa, invite guests to their community center and offer them *zigni* (a spicy stew) served over *injera* (a large, spongy pancake). Kids show good manners by saying "Tu'um!" (Delicious!)

Winter in this mountain city offers a sharp contrast to the dry heat of Eritrea's desert coastline. Some Denver kids learn to ski almost as soon as they can walk, snowplowing downhill through fluffy powder. Families head for the hills in the summertime, too, to enjoy the area's fantastic camping, hiking, biking, and rafting. If you like the great outdoors, Denver's got something just for you.

A Denver boy befriends a polar bear cub

## More about
# Denver

**Founded:** 1858

**Total population:** 554,636

**Youth population:** 135,816

**Nickname:** Mile-High City

**Some languages heard in Denver:** Italian, Korean, Spanish, Tigrinya, Vietnamese

**Sister cities:** Chennai, India; Ulaanbaatar, Mongolia

# NEW HAVEN

Making the most of a summer day

Learning on board the
Freedom Schooner *Amistad*

Imagine sailing back in time to take part in a historic struggle for freedom! New Haven witnessed a dramatic event in 1839. Fifty-three Africans had been kidnapped from West Africa. When they arrived in Cuba, destined to become slaves, their captors loaded them aboard the ship *La Amistad* to take them to a plantation. The Africans, led by Sengbe Pieh (also known as Joseph Cinque), seized control of *La Amistad* and demanded that the crew sail for Africa.

But at night the crew secretly steered the ship north. The U.S. Navy eventually took custody of the zigzagging ship in Long Island Sound, and the Africans were jailed in New Haven. Members of New Haven's black Congregational church helped fight for the Africans' freedom, and former president John Quincy Adams defended the captives before the U.S. Supreme Court. In a landmark decision, the Court ruled that the Africans were born free, and in November 1841, thirty-five survivors returned to Africa. This event took place years before slavery was abolished in this country!

New Haven is now home port for Freedom Schooner *Amistad*, a ship built to look like the original. On this floating classroom, kids work with the crew to raise the sails and help navigate the ship. They discuss the meanings of freedom and the things they can do to make the world a better place.

Kids can taste a bit of history in New Haven's Little Italy. In 1900 Italian immigrant Frank Pepe cooked up the country's first brick-oven pizza. In 1925 he established his pizzeria in the heart of the city's Italian neighborhood. Today customers still line up for the world-famous pizza at Pepe's Pizzeria Napoletana.

Fledgling violinists get excited about music

Another New Havener, Charles Goodyear, also made history with his invention. Have you ever wondered how you came to ride on rubber tires or run in shoes with bouncy rubber soles? For years Goodyear experimented with rubber, a plant material that is bone hard in winter and sticky soft in summer. He discovered a process that weatherproofed it. The discovery, vulcanization, eventually led to the manufacture of rubber automobile tires, sneaker soles, and many other products we use today.

A flounce of the skirt signals the start of the Colombian Cumbia folk dance

## More about
## New Haven

**Founded:** 1784

**Total population:** 123,626

**Youth population:** 37,502

**Nickname:** Elm City

**Some languages heard in New Haven:** Armenian, Chinese, Hebrew, Italian, Spanish

**Sister cities:** Afula-Gilboa, Israel; Amalfi, Italy

# WILMINGTON

Proudly wearing a traditional Nanticoke outfit

Celebrating the Swedish Sankta Lucia holiday

Legends say the Nanticokes were so powerful that they could stop their enemies just by blowing in their direction. Today descendents of these American Indians live in Delaware, Maryland, and New Jersey. Their culture and stories are highlighted at the Nanticoke Indian Museum near Wilmington.

Preserving their native culture was also important to people from Sweden, who first came to the Wilmington area in the 1600s. To keep Swedish customs alive, they built the Old Swedes Church, one of the oldest churches in the country. They still hold Sankta Lucia (the Swedish Festival of Light) to celebrate the coming of Christmas. During this festival, the eldest girl in each family is accompanied by *stjarngossar* (star boys) and *tomtar* (elves) while she serves traditional Lucia bread, a sweet bread filled with almonds and raisins.

Another traditional celebration is August Quarterly, the country's oldest African American folk festival. Started in 1814 by Bishop Peter Spencer, a former slave, it began as a time for gathering, healing, and worship. Today gospel music and jazz transform the city into a musical feast.

Caribbean Americans in Wilmington have ties to thirty West Indian countries, including the Bahamas and Jamaica. Kids can play in a full-steel orchestra modeled after the world-famous University of Delaware Steel Band. The steel drum, or pan, tradition was invented in Trinidad, where discarded oil barrels were pounded and shaped into melodic instruments. Unlike most other drums that only produce a rhythm, musicians can actually play tunes on the pans. Kids in Wilmington also enjoy cricket, a sport popular in the Caribbean, in which players hit a ball with a flat, paddlelike bat.

One of the fastest-growing groups in Wilmington comes from India. The local Hindu temple and community hall hosts activities for fourteen distinct Indian cultures. Kids can study hatha yoga, a centuries-old form of exercise that calms both body and mind. Some girls train hard in the

Winning over the crowd
at the August Quarterly

Families from South Asia add to
Wilmington's mix of cultures

*odissi*, a classical dance from Orissa, a state
in eastern India. Other kids have fun doing
the *ras*, a Gujarati dance from western
India, as they keep time on percussion
sticks called *dandias*.

## More about
# Wilmington

**Founded:** 1638

**Total population:** 72,664

**Youth population:** 20,790

**Nickname:** Chemical Capital of the World

**Some languages heard in Wilmington:**
Creole, Gujarati, Hindi, Oriya, Swedish

**Sister cities:** Kalmar, Sweden; Osogbo,
Nigeria

# WASHINGTON

Walking along the black granite wall of the Vietnam Veterans Memorial

Posing before a classic D.C. backdrop, the Capitol Building

President Abraham Lincoln, nineteen feet tall and carved from marble, watches the sun balance atop the Washington Monument. Close by, Congress meets in the Capitol to represent the people and write the laws of the United States. Washington, D.C., the capital of the United States, is filled with monuments, libraries, and museums that present the history and stories of the nation.

The diversity of the country can be found in the people of Washington. Some families have lived there for centuries, while others have been there just a few weeks. Kids whose families have roots in Algeria, Fiji, and Luxembourg go to school with children from Vietnam and Ecuador.

Kids in D.C. can experience sights, sounds, and smells from around the world. Every year the Folk Life Festival features different cultures, highlighting performers like Haitian *krik krak* storytellers and Azerbaijani musicians. Each spring Japanese cherry trees bloom around the Jefferson Memorial. Giant pandas from China live in the National Zoo, where their Asian elephant neighbors make a big orange mess at the annual Pumpkin Stomp. At Smithsonian

favorites such as the National Museum of the American Indian and the National Air and Space Museum, visitors can view exhibits up close and plunge headlong into learning about art, history, science, and cultures from around the globe.

Theater novices become pros at the Kennedy Center

The arts are all over Washington. The John F. Kennedy Center for the Performing Arts partnered with seven D.C. public schools to mount a production of *Into the Woods, Jr.*, an adaptation of a musical by Stephen Sondheim. Kids from a wide variety of backgrounds, many of whom had never been to the theater, worked together with professionals to design costumes and build sets. They auditioned for parts, filled all the roles, marketed the show, and pulled off a first-class production. The experience helped many of the kids gain new confidence.

Pink cherry blossoms mean spring is here

## More about
# Washington, D.C.

**Founded:** 1790

**Total population:** 572,059

**Youth population:** 135,806

**Nickname:** D.C.

**Some languages heard in Washington:** Amharic, Arabic, Bulgarian, Farsi, Fijian

**Sister cities:** Beijing, China; Dakar, Senegal

# MIAMI

Wolfing down some delicious cheese fries

Zipping down the tunnel slide

What are snowbirds doing in warm, sunny Miami, Florida? There are beaches, skyscrapers, pastel houses, and palm trees, but no snow anywhere! "Snowbird" is a nickname for a person who flees cold winters for sun-baked southern climates. Often snowbirds are retired senior citizens who migrate with the birds—south in the winter and north in the summer.

Miami is also popular with people from tropical countries. These immigrants, new and old, have brought rich traditions to their neighborhoods. Little Havana, the center of the Cuban American community, is home to Calle Ocho, the largest Latino celebration in the United States. Miami's Cuban American musicians, like Grammy winner Gloria Estefan, have greatly influenced American music. Ifé-Ilé, a famous dance troupe, teaches Miami kids Cuban dances like the mambo and the conga, along with ballet and hip-hop.

"Alo!" is heard in Little Haiti, a neighborhood of Haitian Americans who come from the island nation east of Cuba. Kids learn about Haiti's history at the Libreri Mapou

Cultural Center. They study the Haitian Creole language and traditional dances like the hip-twisting *banda*. And they learn about heroes like Marleine Bastien, who helps Haitian families adjust to life in Miami and fights against all types of discrimination. Her defense of human rights has earned her many prestigious honors and awards.

Brazilian American kids say that Miami is "uma cidade divertide e quente" (a fun and hot city)! The bilingual Ada Merritt Elementary School invites Miami children to study Portuguese, Brazil's national language. These kids study Brazilian arts along with math, science, and reading. Brazil, which lies south of the equator, takes up half of South America.

Far from the Arctic Circle, you can hear echoes of the ancient Icelandic language. Icelandic American kids agree with their neighbors that Miami is "falleg og skemmtileg borg" (a beautiful and fun city). At the Icelandic American Association of South Florida, kids can learn to speak Icelandic and practice Iceland's customs. On Christmas Eve they eat a festive rice pudding called *hrisgrjonagrautur* (REES-gree-oh-naw-groy-tur). The one who finds a pecan hidden in the pudding gets a special present.

Visiting the flamingos at Miami's Metrozoo

Hips sway to Cuban beats

## More about
# Miami

**Founded:** 1896

**Total population:** 362,470

**Youth population:** 87,705

**Nickname:** Gateway to the Americas

**Some languages heard in Miami:** Haitian Creole, Icelandic, Portuguese, Seminole, Yiddish

**Sister cities:** Agadir, Morocco; Buenos Aires, Argentina

# ATLANTA

Just hanging out in Georgia

In 1837 a railroad surveyor pounded a stake into a forest clearing. Within a few years the area blossomed into a busy town. By the time of the Civil War, Atlanta was one of the most important cities in the South. In 1864 Union forces burned Atlanta, destroying two-thirds of the city's stores and homes. But the residents rebuilt quickly. The next year about 150 stores were already open for business!

After the Civil War many African Americans settled in Atlanta. By 1900 they made up about half the city's population. Many lived in the Sweet Auburn district, a vibrant community where businesses thrived. Today black students still attend nearby Morehouse and Spelman colleges and several other historically black colleges where they learn to become civic leaders.

Do you know why most schools are closed the third Monday in January? It's Martin Luther King, Jr,. Day! This famous civil rights leader was born in the Sweet Auburn district. He won the Nobel Peace Prize in 1964 for his efforts to win equality for all people. Not everyone agreed with Dr. King's vision. In 1968 he was assassinated in Memphis, Tennessee. Today many people visit his tomb at the King Center in Atlanta. Nearby stands the Ebenezer Baptist Church, where Dr. King, his father, and his grandfather preached.

Since Atlanta's founding, waves of immigrants from around the world have come to work in its factories, cotton

These kids think day camp is worth smiling about!

warehouses, and textile mills. In 1891 Candler's Drug Store, a small Atlanta business, sold a tonic called Coca-Cola that was said to cure headaches. Coca-Cola has since grown into a multinational corporation headquartered in Atlanta. The city is home to other major companies like United Parcel Service (UPS), Home Depot, and CNN, television's first twenty-four-hour news channel.

Atlanta is sometimes called the World's Next Great International City. Along Buford Highway, one of the most diverse streets in the Southeast, are Vietnamese nail boutiques, Chinese herb stores, and Spanish greeting-card shops. Atlantans welcomed athletes and visitors from more than 190 nations when they hosted the Olympic Games in 1996.

Resting after a long bike ride

Exploring the enormous Chinatown Square Mall

## More about
# Atlanta

**Founded:** 1837

**Total population:** 416,474

**Youth population:** 109,123

**Nicknames:** Hotlanta, World's Next Great International City

**Some languages heard in Atlanta:** Arabic, Chinese, Japanese, Spanish, Vietnamese

**Sister cities:** Brussels, Belgium; Montego Bay, Jamaica

# HONOLULU

Snorkeling with a green sea turtle

A cowgirl rides through
the Aloha Week Parade

Big schools of red *aweoweo* fish have returned to the Pacific Ocean around Honolulu, on the island of Oahu. Native Hawaiians believe the presence of these fish means big changes are about to happen.

Much has already changed in this state capital. At one time Honolulu was the center of the kingdom of Hawaii. In the 1700s Europeans, and later Americans, built sugar plantations on Native Hawaiian lands. The last ruler of Hawaii, Queen Liliuokalani, worked hard to restore some of her people's rights, but in 1895 the newcomers claimed Hawaii for themselves. Hawaii eventually became the fiftieth state of the Union in 1959.

Today schools like the Halau Ku Mana charter school keep Native Hawaiian culture alive by teaching its language, history, and way of life. Kids learn by monitoring the health of a coral reef or by growing Native Hawaiian foods. They help build Polynesian voyaging canoes, learning math, construction, and navigation skills. Kids also compete in outrigger canoe racing. Some Hawaiians hope that children will help bring about the changes promised by the return of the *aweoweo*.

Throughout the 1800s many Portuguese escaped poverty by coming to Honolulu, where they adapted to a new life. Some worked on sugar plantations; others became *paniolos* (Hawaiian cowboys), with skills that rivaled the cowboys of the American West. Kids today can learn to play the ukulele, a Portuguese banjo-like instrument. *Ukulele* means "jumping flea" in Hawaiian and might refer to how quickly a ukulele player's fingers fly over the strings.

Puerto Ricans and Chinese also came to work on Honolulu's plantations, alongside Norwegians and Japanese. In the early 1900s Koreans came to Honolulu to

Girlfriends read together

Splashing around in the Aloha State

work, too. At the Halla Pai Huhm Korean Dance Studio, kids learn traditional Korean dances along with newer ones that blend Eastern and Western styles. The *yang sando mambo* features Korean music and dancers in ballet tutus, and it was influenced by the mambo, a Cuban dance!

Honolulu kids can mambo down to the ocean to surf. The sport of surfing was made famous by Olympic champion Duke Paoa Kahanamoku, a Native Hawaiian. Long before kids around the world were using boogie boards, Hawaiians were gliding over the *kai* (sea).

Oahu, Hawaii's most populous island, is home to many Native Hawaiians

## More about
# Honolulu

**Founded:** around 1100

**Total population:** 371,657

**Youth population:** 80,349

**Nickname:** Sheltered Bay

**Some languages heard in Honolulu:** Chinese, Hawaiian, Korean, Portuguese, Spanish

**Sister cities:** Baku, Azerbaijan; Hiroshima, Japan

# BOISE

Fiddling to folk music at the National Oldtime Fiddlers' Contest and Festival

Boise students take a break from the books

"Les bois!" Boise may have gotten its name from nineteenth-century French Canadian fur trappers who came upon the tree-lined river and exclaimed, "The woods!" in French. Boise's nickname is the City of Trees. This clean and green state capital has more than fifty parks where people can play, dance, and celebrate. At the Red River Powwow Association, Paiute, Lakota, and Nez Perce kids learn to compete in the colorful Fancy Dance. Kids fly in the air with acrobatic footwork, but when the music stops, both feet must be on the ground or the dancer is eliminated.

Dance is also a big part of El Dia de los Niños, a Latin American holiday that celebrates children. Idaho was the first U.S. state to proclaim this holiday. During the festivities the young members of the Hispanic Folkloric Dancers help keep a variety of cultures alive by performing traditional dances from Veracruz, Chiapas, and other Mexican states. They have even danced for Idaho's governors.

Another popular Boise dance troupe is Oinkari, whose name means "those who do it with their feet" in the Basque language. Kids join in the dancing at the annual Basque San Inazio Festival. Basque people first came to Boise in the 1800s from the Pyrenees Mountains of Spain and France. In Boise they soon became experts at the only job available, sheepherding.

Newcomers have added different energies to the city. Boise offers a safer home to boys and girls from Afghanistan, a country just emerging from many years of civil war. Afghan kids excel in their new environment at home and at school. At special events, kids dance the *Atan*, an Afghan folk dance.

Boise's many Welsh Americans dance and recite verses as part of their Noson Lawen (Merry Evening) celebrations. Many Americans are of Welsh descent. In fact, all but one of the first six U.S. presidents had Welsh ancestors. Settlers from Wales tied yellow ribbons around trees to welcome new immigrants from home. Today Americans of all backgrounds tie yellow ribbons around trees while waiting to welcome soldiers returning home.

Ice fishing in the Cascade Reservoir

Leather sandals tied with strips of wool complete this traditional Basque outfit

## More about
# Boise

**Founded:** 1863

**Total population:** 185,787

**Youth population:** 52,938

**Nickname:** City of Trees

**Some languages heard in Boise:** Basque, Nahua, Pashto, Shoshone, Welsh

**Sister cities:** Chita, Russia; Gernika, Spain

# CHICAGO

Tossing a beach ball on Oak Street Beach

Dancing to Polish music at Taste of Polonia

Giant Bert and Ernie kites flap against clear blue skies while kids maneuver homemade kites in saffron, turquoise, and magenta. Nicknamed the "Windy City," Chicago hosts the annual Mayor Daley's Kids and Kites Festival, where kids' spirits soar.

Despite winds that "could strip the fur off a buffalo," this city on the southern shore of Lake Michigan became a popular destination for settlers. Around 1779, Jean Baptiste Point du Sable, who was of Haitian and French ancestry, and Kittihawa (Catherine), his Potawatomi wife, started a trading post on the Chicago River. They traded furs, meat, tools, and other supplies with American Indians, trappers, and settlers. Some historians believe this trading post was the beginning of Chicago, the third largest city in the United States and the biggest in the Midwest.

Immigrants began to pour into the area by boat, wagon, and train to work in meatpacking plants, steel mills, and factories making farm machines. Chicago grew into a city with seventy-seven neighborhoods, each rich with cultural diversity. Today, it has the largest Polish population outside Poland. The city's Ukrainian Village is home to storefronts with signs in Cyrillic (the Ukrainian alphabet) and churches with golden domes. Delis serve cabbage rolls, and bakeries sell *korovay* (wedding bread). This bread, beautifully decorated with birds or flowers, is said to bring good luck when used in wedding ceremonies.

After the Civil War, many freed slaves came to Chicago. During the two World Wars, busloads of southern blacks left poor farms to fill wartime factory jobs. By the 1970s, the city's South Side, where many African Americans had settled, became known as the black capital of America. World-famous musicians like B.B. King and Chuck Berry, writers like Richard Wright, and successful businesspeople got their starts there.

Future soccer stars

Chicago kids have a bonanza of parks—over 550 of them! In Millennium Park kids can zip around the outdoor ice rink during the long ice-skating season. At the Lincoln Park Zoo, kids can get close to cuddly meerkats or view a roomful of two-inch-long hissing cockroaches. Every Halloween, some parks are dressed up with spooky haunted houses and festive pumpkin patches.

Getting soaked in the
Crown Fountain at Millennium Park

## More about
# Chicago

**Founded:** around 1779

**Total population:** 2,896,016

**Youth population:** 844,298

**Nickname:** Windy City

**Some languages heard in Chicago:** Assyrian, Ojibwa, Polish, Tibetan, Ukrainian

**Sister cities:** Casablanca, Morocco; Warsaw, Poland

# FORT WAYNE

Ushering in the Burmese New Year
at the *Thingyan* (Water) festival

Playing Macedonian folk songs

General "Mad Anthony" Wayne got his nickname from his daring military plans. In 1794 he built a fort where three rivers came together. The fort and the city that grew up around it were named after him. In 1795 Miami chief Little Turtle called the area the "glorious gateway to the west." All three rivers lead to the mighty Mississippi River, and across the Mississippi is the American West. Since those early days, Fort Wayne has grown into a diverse city where neighbors pitch in to create a safe place to live.

Fort Wayne is home to a large Macedonian American community. Many Macedonians left their homes in the Balkan States of southeastern Europe in the late 1800s. The immigrants found freedom, security, and jobs in Fort Wayne. Today members of the community help train teachers so kids can learn about Macedonian culture. Folk dances like the *horos* are taught in elementary schools, and music teachers introduce their students to the *gajda* (bagpipe), the *tapan* (a traditional wooden drum), and other Balkan musical instruments.

In the mid-1800s all the members of a Swiss Mennonite church moved from Switzerland to an area near Fort Wayne. They founded Berne to have a safe place to live and worship. The Swiss influence is still strong in Berne. Sweet apple dumplings, big wheel races, and mini-tractor pulls delight kids at the annual Swiss Days Festival. Visitors can tour local furniture factories to see the art of furniture crafting brought from Switzerland.

Dribbling past the defense

Fort Wayne still offers a safe shelter for newcomers. During the 1990s the military generals of Myanmar (formerly Burma) imprisoned people who resisted their rule, and denied them human rights. Hundreds of farmers and resistance fighters fled the country, and many arrived in Fort Wayne. Volunteers helped these immigrants settle in and find jobs and resources. Burmese-speaking children can attend classes to learn English at the local Buddhist temple, a place for community activities as well as worship. More Burmese live in Fort Wayne than in any other city in the United States.

Celebrating the Swiss Days Festival

## More about
# Fort Wayne

**Founded:** 1794

**Total population:** 205,727

**Youth population:** 61,775

**Nicknames:** Summit City, City of Churches

**Some languages heard in Fort Wayne:** Burmese, German, Laotian, Macedonian, Serbian

**Sister cities:** Plock, Poland; Takaoka, Japan

INDIANA

# SIOUX CITY

Getting up close and personal
with Mother Nature

Proudly displaying "Old Glory"

The next time you eat a big bowl of popcorn, think of Sioux City. The area has rich, deep, black soil where golden corn and other crops have flourished for hundreds of years. Farmers sell some of their corn directly to popcorn companies. Much of it is fed to livestock. Sioux City farmers have helped make Iowa one of the top ten states in producing corn, hogs, and cattle.

It takes lots of farmers to grow crops and raise animals. In 1869 the state of Iowa published a booklet urging immigrants to settle in the state. The booklet was translated into many European languages. The publicity campaign worked. Families from countries including Denmark, Holland, and Sweden arrived in Sioux City looking for jobs.

Many came to farm, and more farmers meant more hogs. The increase in hogs led to the development of the city's meatpacking industry. Newcomers from eastern Europe came to work at companies like Armour and Swift. Since 1975 Laotian refugees from Southeast Asia have also found jobs in plants for packing meat and processing honey and poultry. These jobs now attract many immigrants from Latin American countries as well.

Sioux City offers a beautiful environment for all families to live in. But the scenic rivers, high bluffs, and rolling hills were there long before the city was founded, as were many American Indian peoples. Huyana (War Eagle), a Sioux man, lived near present-day Sioux City. He tried, but failed, to protect his people's lands from white settlement. Despite his name, War Eagle favored peace. When he died, local citizens honored him by naming the city after his nation.

Neighborhood friends
in the Hawkeye State

## IOWA

In 1804 explorers Meriwether Lewis and William Clark recorded in their journals descriptions of the beautiful prairie lands they saw. Much of the Great Plains has since been turned into grain fields and pastures. At the Lewis and Clark Interpretive Center, fourth and fifth graders study their environment. The Garden of Discovery project teaches kids about restoring the vast prairies and plants that once existed in the Sioux City area.

Receiving First Holy Communion
at a Catholic church

### More about
# Sioux City

**Founded:** 1854

**Total population:** 85,013

**Youth population:** 25,798

**Nickname:** Successful, Surprising Sioux City

**Some languages heard in Sioux City:** Laotian, Lithuanian, Polish, Russian, Spanish

**Sister city:** Yamanashi City, Japan

# TOPEKA

An in-line skater catches air

Making their way to the top!

Smoke from burning sage carries prayers spoken in the Potawatomi and Kickapoo languages across Topeka. The ceremony prepares the grounds for the annual intertribal powwow, a celebration of life that provides a chance for kids to learn from their American Indian classmates.

Joan Finney, a longtime supporter of American Indian education, was the first governor to include American Indian ceremonies in her inauguration. Her inaugural events in 1991 also included a tribute to pioneer women. Born in Topeka, the state capital, Governor Finney was the first woman and the first Catholic to be elected governor of Kansas.

Some of Topeka's first non–American Indian residents were ethnic Germans from Russia who came to work on the Santa Fe Railroad in the 1870s. They were joined by Greeks, Russians, and Mexicans. These immigrants built churches where traditional songs are still sung in their original languages. Our Lady of Guadalupe Catholic School hosts Fiesta Mexicana as a fund-raiser. Kids jump to Tejano music, cheer for the low-rider car parade, and cool off with *raspas* (snow cones).

Topeka schools teach kids about the different people who live in their city and the history that made it possible for them to go to school together. At one time it was legal to have separate schools for black and white children, but black schools were often not as good as white schools. In 1951 a group of Topeka's African American parents went to court to challenge the law. Their lawsuit was named *Brown v. Board of Education* after Oliver Brown, one of the parents. After a long legal battle, the parents won! In its decision the U.S. Supreme Court declared that school segregation was against the law. The lawyer for the parents was Thurgood Marshall, who later became the first African American to serve on the Supreme Court.

Caring for the pigs on a nearby farm

Today Topeka's once all-black, segregated Monroe School is a National Historic Site and a museum. Kids from every background can volunteer there as Junior Rangers. These young guides help visitors learn about the Fourteenth Amendment to the U.S. Constitution, which guarantees all citizens equal protection under the law.

**KANSAS**

Speeding downhill
on a sunny afternoon

## More about
# Topeka

**Founded:** 1857

**Total population:** 122,377

**Youth population:** 33,075

**Some languages heard in Topeka:**
Arabic, German, Kickapoo, Potawatomi, Spanish

**Sister city:** None

# LOUISVILLE

A junior equestrian enjoys therapeutic horseback riding

If you are reading this book in Braille, it was probably published in Louisville, Kentucky, the world's largest producer of books for the blind. Some visually impaired kids take a break from reading to ride horses at Louisville's Green Hill Therapy Stables. They can also hear horses galloping at breakneck speeds. The city is home to the Kentucky Derby, America's most famous horse race.

Some of the world's fastest horses, ridden by the sport's best jockeys, charge around the racetrack during the mile-and-a-quarter Kentucky Derby. African American jockeys won over half of the Kentucky Derbies before 1910. The best known is Isaac Murphy, the first jockey to be inducted into the Jockey Hall of Fame. Many of the country's early racehorses were also trained by African Americans. Young riders of all abilities travel with their horses to Louisville for the Eastern National 4-H Horse Roundup. Dozens of 4-H teams from across the country compete in events testing their riding skill and knowledge of hippology, the study of horses.

Letting loose at Waterfront Park

People are attracted to Louisville for more than just horses. The Presbyterian Church moved its headquarters to Louisville from New York when a Louisville church elder donated a new center to the church. Muslims from very different places, including Bangladesh, Bosnia, Russia, and Iraq, also call the city home. Their religion, Islam, is the second largest in the world.

World boxing champion Muhammad Ali, one of the greatest athletes who ever lived, is a Muslim who was born and raised in Louisville. The Muhammad Ali Center is a place where kids learn to respect one another and build a world of peace. Ali has always stood up for his beliefs. His magnetic personality, strong political views, and funny rhymes about his opponents made him a star outside the boxing arena as well.

When Louisville teachers Mildred and Patty Hill wrote the melody for "Happy Birthday to You" more than a century ago, they had no idea the song would become famous around the world. Since 1875 another Louisville song has become a classic: "My Old Kentucky Home" is played before every running of the Kentucky Derby.

Staging a play in American Sign Language

KENTUCKY

Families of South Asian heritage call Louisville home

## More about
# Louisville

**Founded:** 1778

**Total population:** 256,231

**Youth population:** 68,274

**Nickname:** Falls City

**Some languages heard in Louisville:** Albanian, Arabic, Bosnian, Farsi, Urdu

**Sister cities:** Montpellier, France; Tamale, Ghana

# NEW ORLEANS

Strumming a washboard at
the French Quarter Festival

**M**uffulettas, *baleadas*, and *gumbo* are fun words to say. The foods they name taste even better! These yummy dishes were created by mixing the traditions of the different peoples who live in the river-port city of New Orleans, Louisiana.

*Muffulettas* are big, round sandwiches stuffed with Italian meats and olive salad. Italians from Sicily created this dish to feed hungry dockworkers in the early 1900s. These early immigrants helped build the city. Today Sicilians make up one-sixth of New Orleans's population.

*Baleadas* are thick, warm tortillas smeared with fried red beans, crumbled cheese, and Honduran cream. They are as big as Frisbees! Many Hondurans came to New Orleans to work in the fruit industry, and they brought the recipe for *baleadas* with them. Today more Hondurans live in New Orleans than in any other U.S. city.

*Gumbo* is an international stew developed by African American cooks in New Orleans almost two centuries ago. The African vegetable okra, Choctaw Indian filé powder, and Spanish and French seasonings spice up the dish. African Americans also cooked up the first jazz music in New Orleans and then sent it up the Mississippi River to other cities. Jazz legend Louis Armstrong was born in New Orleans.

Collecting colorful beads at Mardi Gras

New Orleans is known worldwide for its Mardi Gras festivities. Early French colonists brought the Mardi Gras (Fat Tuesday) holiday to America in the 1700s. This joyful celebration occurs just before the solemn period of Lent. Kids look forward to colorful parades and special foods like king cakes. The lucky person who finds a miniature doll hidden in a king cake becomes king or queen for the day.

Cajuns, another group central to the flavor of New Orleans, trace their ancestry to French Canadians who were expelled from Canada by the British. Many live in

Shelling crayfish on the Bayou

the rural bayou areas outside the city. *Piquante* means "to prick" in French, and spicy Cajun alligator stew called *piquante* does just that to tastebuds! Descendants of the original French, Spanish, African, and Caribbean peoples are called Creoles. Like the Cajuns, they are famous for their delicious, spicy food.

In 2005 Hurricane Katrina almost destroyed New Orleans. But the city's residents and people across the country are working together to rebuild this famous city. In time they hope New Orleans will rise again as a food and cultural center of the world.

Nibbling on a delicious deep-fried beignet

## More about
# New Orleans

**Founded:** 1717

**Total population:** 484,674

**Youth population:** 145,710

**Nicknames:** Big Easy, Crescent City

**Some languages heard in New Orleans:** Creole, French, Hindi, Italian, Spanish

**Sister cities:** Juan-les-Pins, France; Pointe-Noire, Congo

A musical funeral procession for trumpeter Al Hirt

**LOUISIANA**

51

# PORTLAND

Taking the helm at the
Children's Museum of Maine

Learning to conserve wildlife
at Maine Audubon

**D**awn lights up the harbor in Portland, Maine, before almost anywhere else in the United States. This city on the North Atlantic coast is just about as far east as you can get in the United States. Most American Indians in the Portland area are Wabanaki (whose name means "People of the Dawnland").

Over the past four hundred years, people from almost every continent have sailed to Maine. Some of today's African American Portlanders are seventh-generation mariners. Their ancestors caulked ships and made sails. Some now work on commercial and naval ships, in shipyards, or as fishermen.

Irish immigrants, refugees from the Great Famine of the 1840s, found work as longshoremen in Portland. The Maine Irish Heritage Center celebrates their stories and the many Irish contributions to American life. At the center's language classes you might be greeted with "Dia duit," which means "hello" or "God be with you" in Gaelic.

Many of the city's early residents were Catholic. James Augustine Healy (1830–1900) was the country's first African American Catholic priest and bishop. He spoke French fluently and required his priests to be bilingual so they could help Portland's French-speaking people. He is remembered as the children's bishop because of his kindness to children.

Today cargo and cruise ships displaying flags from many countries visit Portland's busy harbor. New Portland residents also arrive on planes. Some children and their families come from war-torn countries, like Azerbaijan.

Portland's Center for Grieving Children helps the kids express their emotions with art. Through laughter and storytelling, kids sprout new hopes and beginnings.

Mogadishu, a seaport in Somalia, has also been at the center of fierce civil conflicts. Somali kids feel much safer in Portland, where they attend school with kids from Russia, Uganda, Albania, and Rwanda. Portland's new families have helped rebuild the city's downtown.

Gazing at the Portland Head Light lighthouse

At the Center for Cultural Exchange, artists from around the country and the world teach everything from Brazilian *capoeira* (a martial art) to Indonesian puppet making. People may travel thousands of miles to get to Portland, but at the Center for Cultural Exchange, kids travel the world without leaving the city!

Buddies at the Center for Grieving Children

**M A I N E**

## More about
## Portland

**Founded:** 1845

**Total population:** 64,249

**Youth population:** 13,519

**Nicknames:** Forest City, Hill City

**Some languages heard in Portland:** Acholi, Arabic, Khmer, Somali, Spanish

**Sister cities:** Arkhangelsk, Russia; Cap Haitien, Haiti

# BALTIMORE

Coming face-to-face with marine life at the aquarium

Harmonizing with the Children's Chorus of Maryland

Every spring Baltimore kids share a meal with elephants. To celebrate the arrival of the circus, kids and elephants march from the Baltimore Arena to the two hundred-year-old Lexington Market for a stand-up lunch. Thousands of oranges, apples, and bananas are gobbled up in a flash! Sometimes the group jigs along to Irish and Scottish bagpipe music played by the Baltimore City Pipe Band.

You can hear many different kinds of music in the two hundred neighborhoods that make up Baltimore. Dutch, Germans, and European Jews brought songs in many languages to the city. During Jewish religious services, a special singer called a cantor leads the congregation in prayer. Today Baltimore bands perform lively Jewish soul music called klezmer. It has roots in Hungarian, Russian, Romanian, Arabic, and Roma music.

Roma people have traveled the world for more than a thousand years. Some of Baltimore's Roma families came from Kosovo, Hungary, or Spain more than a century ago. They brought with them songs that tell the history of their people. Roma families continue to pass along their musical traditions. Kids who master a rapid fingering technique to play the seven-string guitar often had a great-grandparent who played the guitar, too. Today Roma musicians perform toe-tapping music, from traditional flamenco tunes to American jazz.

Baltimore kids can study jazz at the Eubie Blake National Jazz Institute and Cultural Center. Eubie Blake, a world-famous musician and Baltimore resident, taught himself to play the organ by age six and got his first job performing at age fifteen. He composed and played popular, award-winning jazz music for over eighty years.

Racing miniature sailboats
in the Inner Harbor

At Christmas time Puerto Rican kids dance along the streets of Baltimore in small groups of *parranderos* (carolers). They play *bomba y plena* music on *cuatros* (guitar-like instruments) and maracas at the doors of family and friends. The holiday season ends with El Dia de Los Reyes (Three Kings Day), a Latin American celebration when kids receive presents to symbolize the three wise men's gifts to the baby Jesus. Baltimore kids also party to Peruvian *chicha* tunes and the music of Salvadoran bands called *chanchonas* during Latino Fest, when the city celebrates the cultures of more than twenty South and Central American countries.

Proud residents of Charm City

### More about
# Baltimore

**Founded:** 1797

**Total population:** 651,154

**Youth population:** 183,207

**Nickname:** Charm City

**Some languages heard in Baltimore:** Hebrew, Romani, Spanish, Telugu, Ukrainian

**Sister cities:** Gbarnga, Liberia; Luxor, Egypt

# BOSTON

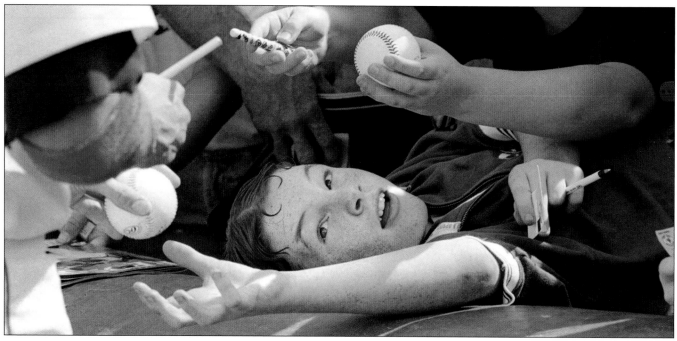

A devoted Red Sox fan struggles to get an autograph at Fenway Park

The front stoop makes a great reading spot in Beantown

The Massachuset people once inhabited a marshy peninsula, now called Boston, and their descendants still live nearby. European fishermen and explorers began arriving in the area in the late 1500s. By the 1620s, Pilgrims and Puritans from England recognized the advantages of this site along the Massachusetts Bay and began to settle there. The newcomers cut down the crests of Boston's hills and used dirt and rock to fill in salt marshes and mudflats. Since 1630 landfill projects have more than tripled Boston's original size!

As the size of the city grew, so did its Irish community. The first Irish people came to Boston, now the state capital, in the late 1600s. Their numbers jumped to over one hundred thousand during the mid-1800s, when immigrants fled Ireland's potato famine. Hungry children worked alongside adults in Boston's textile mills and factories. In time Irish people achieved social and economic success. John F. Kennedy was a congressman from Boston before becoming the thirty-fifth U.S. president. Some call Boston the Irish American capital of the United States.

Like the Irish, Italians came to escape poverty. Many arrived at the turn of the twentieth century. At first they took backbreaking jobs, but many Italians soon prospered. In 1993 Thomas Menino became Boston's first Italian American mayor. Mayor Menino and all Bostonians celebrated in 2004 when the Boston Red Sox won baseball's World Series for the first time since 1918. The Red Sox play ball at Fenway Park, the oldest and smallest major-league baseball stadium still in operation.

Boston is home to many famous colleges and universities. Not far from Fenway Park sits Boston University. In nearby Cambridge are Harvard University and the Massachusetts Institute of Technology.

On the other side of the city is Dorchester, where Portuguese is spoken on the busy streets, and restaurants serve cod fritters and *bolachas* (cookies). In the late 1800s Portuguese-speaking Cape Verdeans came from islands off the West African coast. Expert seamen, many found jobs on dangerous whaling ships. Today many succeed as teachers, lawyers, and doctors. More than 140 languages are spoken in the neighborhoods of Boston, which continue to attract new immigrants every year.

Make way for ducklings!

MASSACHUSETTS

Exploring the beach at low tide

## More about
## Boston

**Founded:** 1630

**Total population:** 589,141

**Youth population:** 141,951

**Nicknames:** Beantown, Cradle of Liberty

**Some languages heard in Boston:** Arabic, Irish Gaelic, Italian, Portuguese, Vietnamese

**Sister cities:** Padua, Italy; Sekondi-Takoradi, Ghana

57

# DEARBORN

Hometown boys parade down the street

Hanging out with friends in front of
St. Sarkis Armenian Apostolic Church

Long before Dearborn, Michigan, was a city, it was part of the Odawa (Ottawa) homelands. *Odawa* means "people who are home anywhere." Their leader, Chief Pontiac, united American Indian peoples to help protect their territory. Today American Indians as well as people from many places in the world call Dearborn home.

In 1903 the Ford Motor Company began mass-producing affordable cars in Dearborn factories. High wages drew workers from all over the country and western Europe. Scots, Italians, and Poles settled around the Ford plant. Nearby Wyandotte has a traditional Polish community where many kids attend Catholic schools. They learn the Polish language along with reading, math, and science.

Dearborn has one of the country's largest Arab American populations. Lebanese were the first to arrive, seeking employment in the auto industry. Most Dearborn Arab American families trace their roots to Lebanon, Iraq, and Yemen. Some are of Syrian and Palestinian heritage. Chaldeans (Iraqi Catholics) attend church services given in Arabic, English, and Aramaic, an ancient language believed to have been spoken by Jesus.

Five times a day, calls to worship echo from mosques, Muslim places of worship. These calls are similar to bells ringing before church services. Many Dearborn kids are Muslim, or followers of Islam, one of the world's largest faiths. Although Yemenis, Jordanians, and Lebanese may speak slightly different versions of Arabic, they worship together. Some kids attend Islamic school, but most go to the city's public schools.

In the Maples Elementary School Arabic Ensemble, kids keep the rhythm on *derbeki* (hourglass-shaped hand drums) and tambourines, while others sing and dance. The ensemble performs music of various

Carving jack-o'-lanterns for Halloween

Middle Eastern countries. After practice, members help each other with homework. Some kids work on the school newspaper and aspire to follow in the footsteps of Helen Thomas, who grew up in the area. A journalist and Lebanese American, she covered the White House for over fifty years and asked tough questions of eight U.S. presidents! Thomas set high standards and opened doors for women in many areas of journalism.

Drumming for the Maples
Elementary School Arabic Ensemble

## More about
# Dearborn

**Founded:** 1786

**Total population:** 97,775

**Youth population:** 29,649

**Nickname:** Hometown of Henry Ford

**Some languages heard in Dearborn:**
Albanian, Arabic, Bengali, Chaldean, Polish

**Sister city:** Qana, Lebanon

MICHIGAN

# MINNEAPOLIS-ST. PAUL

Piling up in the snow

Waving to the crowd during the Mexican Cinco de Mayo parade

Minneapolis and St. Paul are called the Twin Cities, but they are not identical! St. Paul is the state capital, but Minneapolis is bigger. These neighboring cities face each other across the Mississippi River.

Both cities have long attracted immigrants. Starting in the 1860s Swedish immigrants came for jobs in railroads, mills, and wealthy homes, where thousands of women worked as maids. By 1900 the Twin Cities had the second-largest Swedish population in America.

Since the late 1970s the Twin Cities have welcomed new Asian immigrants, among them Hmong refugees from Laos. The Hmong sided with the United States during the Vietnam War. When the United States pulled out of Vietnam, many Hmong fled their mountain homes. Thousands lived in Thailand's refugee camps for years before they reached safety in the Twin Cities. Because Hmong have a strong sense of family, relatives who had settled in other U.S. cities gradually joined the Twin Cities community. Today St. Paul's East Side has the largest Hmong neighborhood in the nation.

The Twin Cities have also attracted Somalis from East Africa. Most of these families come from rural villages, but they quickly learn to use modern gadgets like cell phones and washers and dryers. Some teachers encourage Somali children to tell stories from their culture's rich oral tradition.

To better tell stories popular in the Twin Cities, libraries and schools have developed bilingual books for the new communities. Kids can read *Tus Tub Rog Thiab Tus Zaj* (The Knight and the Dragon) by Tomie de Paola and over fifteen other books in the White Hmong language, the most common dialect spoken by Hmong people. Minneapolis libraries offer storytelling hours in Hmong and Somali, and one St. Paul branch library presents stories in American Sign Language.

Many organizations extend helping hands to new neighbors to make sure they have clothing, food, and housing. They also offer after-school tutoring for kids, and classes for adults in computers, American citizenship, and English. Minneapolis and St. Paul may be two of the coldest cities in the U.S., but their residents offer a warm welcome that makes newcomers feel right at home.

Kids from the Hmong American community enjoy a game of football

**MINNESOTA**

## More about
# Minneapolis-St. Paul

**Founded:** 1867 (Minneapolis); 1854 (St. Paul)

**Total population:** 382,618 (Minneapolis); 287,151 (St. Paul)

**Youth population:** 98,304 (Minneapolis); 87,825 (St. Paul)

**Nickname:** Twin Cities

**Some languages used in Minneapolis and St. Paul:** American Sign Language, Hmong, Ojibwa, Somali, Swedish

**Sister cities:** Uppsala, Sweden (Minneapolis); Nagasaki, Japan (St. Paul)

Practicing Swedish folk dance steps

# CLARKSDALE

Strumming and picking at the Delta Blues Museum

Taking a turn through a cotton field

In Clarksdale, Mississippi, some kids have got the blues. The Delta blues are a truly original American form of music. Born in Clarksdale and nearby towns, the blues sprang from songs and hollers sung by slaves in cotton and tobacco fields. Blues musicians used foot-stomping music to express their heartache about poverty, segregation, and destructive floods.

In the Delta Blues Museum Art and Education Program, kids work with master blues musicians to learn to play guitars, keyboards, harmonicas, or drums. Others sing the blues. The best of the young musicians perform in bands throughout the South. They dress in suits and ties, just like professional blues musicians. If the group gets paid, each kid gets a share of the fee.

Each spring guitar chords and the voices of blues musicians mix with the rumble of motorcycles at the annual Crossroads Bikes and Blues festival. For several days families camp close to the Expo Center where bike judging and games take place. Older kids get to do chores for the bikers.

Clarksdale lies in the Lower Mississippi Delta, a huge region stretching over seven states. Rich, black soil makes it ideal for growing soybeans and cotton. After the Civil War thousands of freed African Americans headed north to work in cities like Chicago, Illinois. Blacks from other parts of Mississippi moved into the area to farm. Plantation owners also brought a small group of Chinese immigrants to work the land.

Eventually many Chinese left farmwork to start grocery stores and other small businesses. Their customers were mainly African Americans who were

Jumping for joy in Clarksdale

not permitted to shop at stores serving whites. The stores became places to hang out, talk, and even find a job. Today Chinese groceries are fading away. Some Chinese American families in Clarksdale now run restaurants that serve stir-fried bok choy and bamboo shoots mingled with southern staples such as Delta catfish and collard greens.

Horsing around on a summer day

## More about
## Clarksdale

**Founded:** 1848

**Total population:** 20,645

**Youth population:** 7,482

**Nickname:** Home of the Blues

**Some languages heard in Clarksdale:** Chinese, French, German, Italian, Spanish

**Sister city:** Notodden, Norway

MISSISSIPPI

# KANSAS CITY

Racing toward the goal

A member of Sinag-Tala prepares to take the stage

Have you ever gotten a letter saying you're an incredible kid? The Absolutely Incredible Kid Day is sponsored by Camp Fire USA, which is based in Kansas City. Adults write letters of love and support to children. Celebrities like Oprah Winfrey, John Travolta, and basketball star Rebecca Lobo ask grown-ups to let kids know how incredible they are.

Kansas City is full of talented kids. Girls in the Sinag-Tala Performing Arts Group of the Filipino Cultural Center perform traditional dances from the Philippines. In one dance about fetching water, girls dance with *bangas* (pots) on their heads. One dancer ends up balancing all the pots!

Incredible kids get together to make music at WeeBop on the Vine, a jazz festival. Some young musicians perform on the stage while others learn about different jazz styles. In fast-paced bebop, artists create complex new sounds as they play. This is called improvisation. Bebop was invented in Kansas City, where jazz greats like Charlie "Bird" Parker and Count Basie got their starts.

Below the bebopping kids is another Kansas City, called SubTropolis! Businesses, warehouses, a post office, and roads are built in limestone caverns the size of thirty-five football stadiums. There is even a natural-science lab called EarthWorks where young scientists study midwestern habitats. In this huge underground school, kids learn how to help animals during fires or droughts.

Kansas City also has an incredible baseball history. Before 1900, African Americans played in the major leagues. But from 1900 to 1945, they were kept from playing because of laws that upheld segregation. The Negro League, formed in Kansas City, gave blacks the

Yukking it up at the Boys & Girls Club

chance to keep playing ball. Negro League teams played all over the United States, Canada, and Latin America. Superstar Jackie Robinson played with the Negro League's Kansas City Monarchs. He later became the first African American to be on a major-league team since 1900. Not only was Robinson an incredible athlete, he was also an influential leader in the struggle for civil and human rights.

## More about
# Kansas City

**Founded:** 1821

**Total population:** 441,545

**Youth population:** 123,407

**Nickname:** City of Fountains

**Some languages heard in Kansas City:** Arabic, Dutch, Spanish, Swahili, Tagalog

**Sister cities:** Arusha, Tanzania; Freetown, Sierra Leone

Exploring the underground world of EarthWorks

MISSOURI

65

# BUTTE

Sharing a secret on the prairie near Butte

Young engineers show
off their latest invention

In 1882 Marcus Daly, an Irish immigrant, was working in a silver mine in Butte (BYOOT). While mining for silver three hundred feet underground, he discovered a vein of copper fifty feet wide. Daly bought the huge copper mine just as the demand for copper skyrocketed. Copper wiring was essential for electricity and telephones, two major technological advances of the late 1800s.

Butte is located in the northern Rocky Mountains. A butte is a high, steep-sided hill. Gold, silver, and copper mines won Butte a reputation as the richest hill on earth. Almost overnight, armies of miners moved into Butte's mining camps. Many of these prospectors from western Ireland called for relatives to join them. By 1900 nearly a quarter of Butte's population was of Irish descent. Today hundreds of Irish last names like Sullivan, Shannon, and O'Brien appear in the Butte phone book.

Some miners migrated to Butte from mines in Nevada and Pennsylvania. Others came from around the world.

A 1918 survey showed that thirty-eight countries were represented in Butte! That made Butte, a booming city of nearly one hundred thousand, one of the most multicultural American cities of the time.

Many Chinese immigrants, mostly men, came to work in the mines. After the gold ran out, most Chinese families moved elsewhere. By the year 2000 just twenty-eight Chinese American families still lived in Butte. To preserve their history, they created the Mai Wah Society. This organization restores old buildings to house public exhibits about Butte's Asian history. The Mai Wah Society cares for Montana's only authentic parade dragon, a gift from the government of Taiwan to the people of Montana.

Today Butte has a population of nearly thirty-four thousand people from many ethnic groups. There are about 150 Serbian families and a small Jewish community that maintains a restored 1903 synagogue. Even though the city is smaller than it was in its mining heyday, it has one of the largest historic districts in the nation. Kids can visit some of the 4,500 historic buildings, which include everything from miners' cottages to mansions.

Kids venture underground at the World Museum of Mining

Leading the procession at Holy Trinity Serbian Orthodox Church

## More about
# Butte

**Founded:** 1864

**Total population:** 33,892

**Youth population:** 9,055

**Nicknames:** Richest Hill on Earth, Copper City

**Some languages heard in Butte:** Finnish, Hebrew, Irish Gaelic, Italian, Serbian

**Sister city:** Altensteig, Germany

# LINCOLN

Kids from many backgrounds
learn together

In 2004, the Kid-Friendly Cities Report Card gave Lincoln, Nebraska, an A+. This state capital is a great place for children to live because the air is clean, neighborhoods are safe, and schools are good. Lincoln has more than eighty parks in which to hike, bike, swim, and fish. Jobs are plentiful, and the cost of living is low.

Families from all over the world have settled in Lincoln, smack in the center of America's heartland. Lincoln even inspires poetry. Ted Kooser, a famous poet who has lived in Lincoln, writes poetry celebrating farmhouses, snowflakes, creamed corn, and other details of small-town life in middle America. He works hard to create poems that everybody can understand, sometimes writing as many as forty drafts of one poem.

Lincoln is named for President Abraham Lincoln, who in 1863 freed all slaves in states rebelling against the Union. In recent years a variety of people have come to Lincoln seeking freedom. The Lincoln Interfaith Council, made up of over twenty religious organizations, is one of many groups that help newcomers settle. The council works to create a "village of kindness." It provides interpreters who help newcomers interview for jobs, enroll kids in schools, make medical appointments, and go grocery shopping. At the city's ESL (English as a second language) classes, students speak almost fifty different languages.

Since 1975 many Vietnamese have settled in this kid-friendly city. In 2004 and 2005, the Lincoln Children's Museum hosted a traveling exhibit on Vietnamese culture. In one part of the exhibit, children gained a sense of everyday life in Vietnam by riding a virtual scooter and

Fifth graders send school supplies to New Orleans after Hurricane Katrina

Performing a praise dance at
Mount Zion Baptist Church

Showing off one of Lincoln's bullfrogs

pretending to sail on a houseboat like those that float on Vietnam's many rivers. Kids also love to check out "My Town," one of the museum's permanent hands-on exhibits. During their visit they can read X rays in the emergency room, become a pilot or a pizza maker, drive a real tractor, produce a TV show, and much more. Whether it's something from down the block or around the world, there's a lot to discover in Lincoln!

Ready for a header in Green Woods Park

## More about
# Lincoln

**Founded:** 1867

**Total population:** 225,581

**Youth population:** 61,783

**Nickname:** Star City

**Some languages heard in Lincoln:**
Bosnian, Dari, Sudanese, Thai, Vietnamese

**Sister cities:** Khujand, Tajikistan; Taiping, Taiwan

# RENO

Donning traditional Mexican clothes for a special event

Brownie Girl Scouts help care for their environment on May Day

The snowcapped Sierra Nevada Mountains tower over Reno, Nevada. In the spring the snow melts and fills rivers snaking through this dry landscape, providing much-needed water. The area encompasses the ancient homelands of the Paiutes, Washoes, and Shoshones. Today many tribal members live at the Reno-Sparks Indian Colony.

Once poor, this colony is proud of its successful real estate ventures and other businesses. Kids are encouraged to learn about these fields as well as to study their native languages, traditional lifeways, and native arts like willow basket weaving. From picking and curing the willow to the actual weaving, the highly prized willow baskets take months to make.

Mexican American girls in Reno spend years dreaming about their *quinceañera*. The festive occasion marks a girl's fifteenth birthday, when she becomes a woman in the Latino tradition. Celebrations include a mass and can be as fancy as a wedding! Busy *quinceañera* shops, run by Mexican and Guatemalan merchants, supply everything from dresses to decorations. Latino kids in Reno get a head start by learning from professionals in the community how to run these and other ventures and to develop a variety of careers.

Some Korean American kids help out in their families' businesses, answering phones as they do their homework. To keep up with the Korean language, kids attend classes in Korean Presbyterian churches where religious training and Korean traditions are combined.

Italians began to settle in Reno in the late 1800s. They made strides in agriculture and mining and shared their wine-making skills. At the Eldorado Great Italian Festival, toes get stained purple when folks stomp grapes to demonstrate how wine used to be made. And kids' faces get sticky as they gobble gelato, Italy's ice

Practicing new moves at the
Children's Cabinet playground

Performing a
break-dancing freeze

cream. Perhaps Italians truly found *la dolce vita* ("the sweet life") in Reno.

*La dolce vita* is what Wild Horse Annie (Velma Johnston) wanted for the hundreds of mustangs that live around Reno. In the 1950s she and Reno schoolchildren started a campaign to save wild horses and burros from being killed for commercial purposes. Because of their efforts, Congress ended up passing the 1971 Wild Free-Roaming Horses and Burros Act without a nay!

## More about
# Reno

**Founded:** 1868

**Total population:** 180,480

**Youth population:** 47,641

**Nickname:** Biggest Little City in the World

**Some languages heard in Reno:** Basque, Italian, Korean, Paiute, Spanish

**Sister cities:** Guadalupe, Mexico; Wanganui, New Zealand

Getting to know a dinosaur

# MANCHESTER

Who might this Scout be chatting with via ham radio?

A loyal fan supports the local football team

"Bon matin!" "Guid morning!" French, Scots, and sixty other languages once echoed through canyons of redbrick mill buildings in Manchester, New Hampshire's largest city. Located near beautiful Lake Massabesic, Manchester was once one of the largest textile-manufacturing centers in the Northeast.

Textile workers came from Scotland in the 1830s. When these immigrants started to form labor unions to protect workers' rights, mill owners brought in French Canadians to stop the effort. However, the Scots were experts at dyeing and weaving and controlled the dyeing houses right up to the 1960s. Scottish culture is still strong in Manchester, which has the world's largest bagpipe museum.

Soon after the French Canadians settled in Manchester, they founded their own Catholic parishes and a new community called Little Canada. Today the Franco-American Centre celebrates French Canadian culture and Bastille Day. This French independence day is like the American Fourth of July. Recent African immigrants from French-speaking Africa feel at home in Manchester. Some churches hold services in a blend of English, French, Swahili, and Arabic.

Skilled weavers from Uruguay came to Manchester in the 1960s. They were some of the area's first Spanish-speaking textile workers. Today many kids from Latino families grow up speaking English. They can swim and play ball at the Escuelita summer camp, where only Spanish is spoken. Campers get to have fun and practice their Spanish. They also learn about Venezuela, Colombia, and other Latin American countries, which all share a common language but have different customs and histories.

Textile production is no longer the biggest industry in Manchester. The redbrick mills now house families, art, and businesses. People from around the world come to work for the area's banking and technology companies.

Getting extra help from
a local college student

Manchester's Cub and Boy Scouts use airwave technology to create their own worldwide connections. At the Lawrence L. Lee Scouting Museum, Scouts talk on ham radios to kids in Kenya, Japan, Iceland, Australia, and many other places. They learn words in each other's languages and the universal language of ham radio operators. They end a chat by saying "73," ham lingo for "sincere best regards."

Diving into a project at
the annual Latino Festival

## More about
# Manchester

**Founded:** 1722

**Total population:** 107,006

**Youth population:** 28,090

**Nickname:** Queen City

**Some languages heard in Manchester:** Bengali, Cambodian, French, Scots, Spanish

**Sister city:** Neustadt an der Weinstrasse, Germany

# TEANECK

Brownie Girl Scouts wait for the rest of their troop

Demonstrating the right way to knee a soccer ball

Teaneck's name is mysterious. No one knows for sure what it means. It could be a word from the Lenni Lenape language. The area now called Teaneck was originally inhabited by the Hackensacks, one of the Lenni Lenape tribes. Or the name could be Dutch. Dutch settlers arrived in the early 1700s and built houses and farms. Seven of their stone houses, some of the oldest homes in America, still stand in Teaneck.

One thing is sure—Teaneck is a special place. In 1949 the U.S. Army looked at ten thousand communities and chose Teaneck to be a "model American town." A photographer snapped photos showing the fire department in action, work on a sewer project, and hundreds of other activities. An exhibit of these photos traveled to Austria, Germany, and Japan, where people were struggling to rebuild after World War II. The army hoped that Teaneck would be an inspiring example to these countries.

In 1949 Teaneck was mostly white and Christian. Fifteen years later Teaneck was home to many Jewish and African American families. A group of these citizens worked for integrated housing and schools. In 1965 Teaneck became the first town in the nation to voluntarily end segregation in its schools.

Teaneck is home to fifty-two houses of worship. Jews make up about a third of Teaneck's population. Orthodox Jews are attracted by Teaneck's Orthodox synagogues, *mikvah* (ritual bath), kosher restaurants, and nearby yeshivas (religious schools). Jewish law prohibits carrying anything outside the home on the Sabbath, except within a ceremonial boundary called an *eruv*. Such an area is often defined by stringing wires across the tops of utility poles. At least half of Teaneck lies within such an *eruv*.

Ice cream is similar to *kulfee*, a popular Pakistani treat

In recent years Teaneck has welcomed a growing population from South Asia. Two mosques, a religious day school, and Indian and Pakistani restaurants and grocery stores make the town a good place to settle. In 1992 the town elected an Indian mayor, one of the first in the nation. In the past the town has elected Jewish, African American, and female mayors. This reflection of the town's diversity proves how special Teaneck is.

Giggling girls enjoy life in Teaneck

Teaneck has been home to many successful musicians

## More about
# Teaneck

**Founded:** 1895

**Total population:** 39,260

**Youth population:** 11,242

**Some languages heard in Teaneck:**
Chinese, Hebrew, Hindi, Pashto, Spanish

**Sister city:** None

75

# SANTA FE

At a Mexican folk dance

Guatemalan worry dolls brighten up a headband

Santa Fe, located almost seven thousand feet up in the Sangre de Cristo Mountains of New Mexico, is the oldest capital city in the United States. Ancestors of the Pueblo people lived there thousands of years before the Spanish came in 1540. In 1821 a wagon train started trading goods along the Santa Fe Trail, a route from Franklin, Missouri, to Santa Fe. It soon brought a wave of Anglo settlers to the area. Santa Fe has become famous for the way Pueblo, Spanish, and Anglo cultures influence the city's everyday life.

When you walk around Santa Fe, you see many buildings made of adobe, a mixture of sun-dried clay, sand, straw, and water. Even one of the town's McDonald's, painted in shades of pale brown, reflects the adobe style. Hundreds of years ago American Indians near Santa Fe built dwellings that looked a bit like modern apartment buildings. Ten-inch-thick walls kept the interiors cool. The Spanish called these communities *pueblos* (towns). When the Spanish began settling in New Mexico in the 1500s, they built adobe houses, too. But they used building traditions they learned from the Moors and Arabs of North Africa and the Middle East. Their house walls were twice as thick. Church walls could be up to six feet thick! Later, Anglo settlers introduced brick houses, second-story porches, and wood trim around windows.

Hispanic culture is everywhere in Santa Fe. You see it in colorful folk art and clothing. You hear it in Mexican folk music. You taste it in *tortas españolas* (Spanish omelets) and *taquizas* (tacos). Pueblo foods are everywhere,

Showing off indigenous clothing

Feasting on fresh corn on the cob

too. Blue corn chips are tasty with piñon soup. In many courtyards bunches of fiery red chili peppers dry in the sun.

Almost 50 percent of Santa Fe's population is Hispanic (mostly Spanish or Mexican) while 9 percent is Native American. The rest are Anglos, African Americans, Asians, and others who moved to the city or whose families have lived there for generations. They add to Santa Fe's cultural mix, making the city live up to its nickname, the "City Different."

At the National Dance Institute of New Mexico, kids get to dance, dance, dance!

## More about
# Santa Fe

**Founded:** 1607

**Total population:** 62,203

**Youth population:** 14,212

**Nickname:** City Different

**Some languages heard in Santa Fe:** Arabic, Keresan, Spanish, Tewa, Tibetan

**Sister cities:** Bukhara, Uzbekistan; Santa Fe, Spain

# NEW YORK,

**BROOKLYN CHILDREN'S MUSEUM**

BRONX ZOO

MUSEUM OF NATURAL HISTORY

BROOKLYN BRIDGE

**ALPHABET CITY   QUEENS**   BRONX   **LITTLE ITALY**

ROCKEFELLER CENTER SKATING RINK

SUBWAY

EMPIRE STATE BUILDING

## peace

**The incredible diversity of kids in "THE BIG**

# NEW YORK

STATUE OF LIBERTY   B-BOYS   GRAND CENTRAL STATION   CENTRAL PARK   MODEL UNITED NATIONS

MACY'S THANKSGIVING DAY PARADE   SHEA STADIUM

NEW YORK MOSQUE RIVERSIDE CHURCH TEMPLE EMANU-EL

ST. PATRICK'S CATHEDRAL

THE VILLAGE   TAXI!

HARLEM  BROOKLYN  MANHATTAN  **WALL STREET**   CONEY ISLAND   STATEN ISLAND

CHINATOWN  WEST SIDE  **EAST SIDE**  GROUND ZERO

RADIO CITY MUSIC HALL

## More about
# New York City

**Founded:** 1625

**Total population:** 8,008,278

**Youth population:** 2,153,450

**Nicknames:** Big Apple, City That Never Sleeps

**Some languages heard in New York:** More than 140 languages are spoken in this city!

**Sister cities:** Cairo, Egypt; Tokyo, Japan

PPLE"—the largest, busiest city in the United States—is best captured in pictures!

# ASHEVILLE

The Mountain Thunder Cloggers perform to Appalachian bluegrass music

**D**ouble toe step, rock, step. Kids in Asheville grow up clogging at community gatherings. Clogging reaches back to the time when Irish and Scottish immigrants settled in the southern Appalachian Mountains. When they blended their clogging style with Cherokee, African American, and Roma dance moves, they created a unique dance. In Asheville, cloggers move to music played on banjos, fiddles, and guitars. Whether they dance to bluegrass, rock, or hip-hop, you can hear the loud tap-tap of the steel plates attached to the soles of their shoes.

People have been coming to the Asheville area for thousands of years. Cherokees have been living in the Appalachian Mountains since before recorded history. The Spanish and Africans came in the sixteenth century, followed by the Scots and Irish in the 1700s. In the 1880s a railroad was built over the mountains. State prisoners did most of the grueling work with picks and shovels. The railroad opened the area to outsiders. Wealthy city-dwellers from New York and Boston traveled to Asheville's mountains to escape summer heat and the hectic pace of city life, as well as diseases such as tuberculosis.

Many slaves in Asheville worked in the homes of wealthy people and in mountain resorts and mines. After they were freed, African Americans began owning property and businesses. Several hundred black craftsmen built the Young Men's Institute (YMI), which was commissioned by George Vanderbilt, a wealthy industrialist. Opened in 1892, the YMI is now the center of cultural life for local African Americans. Every year, the YMI presents Goombay, a festival celebrating African and Caribbean dance, music, and food. The original Goombay dancers played a skin-covered drum called the gombey. Today some dancers wear high, feathered headdresses and play steel drums.

The center of cultural life for the city's Greek families is the Greek Orthodox church. Greeks began coming to Asheville in the 1920s. The mountains reminded them of their homeland. One family member would open a restaurant and then sponsor another family member's immigration from Greece. Bringing over one person at a time, a Greek family eventually could staff a neighborhood eatery.

Goombay features wonderful music and dance

Curious junior naturalists abound in western North Carolina

Daycare centers are great places to make new friends

## More about
## Asheville

**Founded:** 1794

**Total population:** 68,889

**Youth population:** 15,329

**Nickname:** Land of the Sky

**Some languages heard in Asheville:** Belarusian, Cherokee, Estonian, Greek, Korean

**Sister cities:** San Cristobal de las Casas, Mexico; Vladikavkaz, Russia

NORTH CAROLINA

# FARGO

Slapping the puck around is a favorite activity in Fargo

Children of all backgrounds gather at Cultural Diversity
Resources to build an international community

Millions of bearded bison once thundered across the Great Plains, including the area that is now Fargo, North Dakota. The Dakota people once made their living from buffalo, following the animals as they migrated. But when European settlers arrived, the settlers started to slaughter the buffalo for sport. The Dakotas were forced to settle on nearby reservations. Many of their descendants, along with Assiniboines, Mandans, Ojibwas, and other American Indians live and work in Fargo, North Dakota's largest city.

Some of the first Europeans to settle in Fargo were Scandinavians, Ukrainians, and ethnic Germans from the Black Sea area of Russia. The Hjemkomst (YOM-comst) Festival celebrates Scandinavian cultures. When Icelandic Americans host the event, visitors can sample *mysuostur* (Icelandic whey cheese) and *vinarterta* (prune-filled torte). When Norwegian Americans are the hosts, guests waltz around the dance floor and snack on *potatis klub-kumla* (potato dumplings).

Fargo is a resettlement city for people from as far away as Ethiopia, Vietnam, and Liberia. Refugee resettlement agencies bring people to the city for its jobs, schools, medical care, parks, and low crime. Schools help immigrant students feel at home by serving foods they are used to.

Students enjoy figuring out how many steps it would take to walk to the homelands of each other's ancestors. It is 2,000 miles, or 3,520,000 steps to Mexico, and that's one of the closer countries! Families and friends join in, recording every step they take on pedometers until they have walked the distance to each student's ancestral land.

Some kids who have disabilities can get their exercise in a special place. A unique tree house at the Anne Carlsen Center for Children in nearby Jamestown makes it possible for many of the kids to climb and play. The center's specially designed classrooms also give them a comfortable place to learn and grow. Dr. Anne Carlsen, the center's longtime principal, who retired in 1981, received North Dakota's highest honor, the Theodore Roosevelt Rough Rider Award, for her work. And she, like some of the center's kids, was born without forearms and lower legs.

A cat gets a cuddle during a cold Fargo winter

Getting the feel of an American Indian jingle dress and dance fan

## More about
# Fargo

**Founded:** 1871

**Total population:** 90,599

**Youth population:** 23,046

**Some languages heard in Fargo:**
Amharic, Dakota, Icelandic, Norwegian, Ojibwa

**Sister cities:** Hamar, Norway; Vimmerby, Sweden

**NORTH DAKOTA**

# CINCINNATI

Look art straight in the face at the Cincinnati Art Museum

Kids meet a fellow Ohioan—a penguin!—at the Cincinnati Zoo

Celebrating Id-al-Fitr, the most important Muslim holiday

Three-foot-tall winged pigs stand atop thirty-foot columns overlooking Cincinnati's riverfront. The flying pigs celebrate the years in the 1800s when Cincinnati was the world's major pork-processing center. For a while the city was even nicknamed Porkopolis.

Cincinnati owes much of its growth to the many hardworking German immigrants who settled in a neighborhood they called Over-the-Rhine. A canal that once flowed there reminded them of Germany's Rhine River. By 1890 Cincinnati was teeming with German culture: there were over thirty German-language publications and dozens of churches, synagogues, social clubs, and beer gardens. Street and business signs were printed in German.

After the United States entered World War I against Germany in 1917, anti-German feelings squelched Cincinnati's German American culture. Street signs were changed to English. German books were removed from public libraries, German American teachers were fired, and the language was banned in schools. Decades of effort eventually brought back some German American culture in Greater Cincinnati, where almost fifty percent of the population is German American.

During the early and mid-1800s many African Americans escaped slavery in the South by way of the Underground Railroad. Neither underground nor a railroad, it was a secret escape route for runaway slaves. They reached Cincinnati by crossing the Ohio River and hid in attics, cellars, churches, and woods as they made their way to free northern states or Canada. Cincinnati's National Underground Railroad Freedom Center celebrates runaway slaves like Harriet Tubman and white

Kids and grown-ups participate
in the Freedom Walk

abolitionists like John Rankin, both of whom helped operate the Underground Railroad. Some free blacks and former slaves settled in the city. African Americans now make up about 43 percent of the population.

As lumber mills and coal mines close in the nearby Appalachian Mountains, families with roots in Kentucky and Tennessee have moved to Cincinnati in search of jobs. The Urban Appalachian Council trains teachers so they better understand the rich mountain heritage of music, storytelling, folk art, and crafts. The council runs schools for teens and adults trying to earn high-school diplomas. It also helps preserve Appalachian traditions like quilting, soap making, wood carving, and playing bluegrass music.

Along with quilting and basket weaving,
needlepoint is a treasured Appalachian craft

## More about
# Cincinnati

**Founded:** 1788

**Total population:** 331,285

**Youth population:** 92,586

**Nickname:** Queen City

**Some languages heard in Cincinnati:** Arabic, German, Italian, Russian, Spanish

**Sister cities:** Harare, Zimbabwe; Munich, Germany

# TAHLEQUAH

Singing with the Cherokee National Youth Choir

Kids of every culture appreciate curious cats

Tahlequah (TAL-uh-kwah), the oldest town in Oklahoma, is also the capital of the Cherokee Nation. Long before Europeans came to America, American Indian nations governed themselves. Today U.S. law recognizes them as sovereign nations, but they are also part of the United States.

Cherokees originally lived in the southeastern part of the United States. Then gold was discovered on Cherokee lands. In the bitter winter of 1838, government troops forced twenty thousand Cherokee men, women, and children to march hundreds of miles to Indian Territory, present-day Oklahoma. Thousands died on what is called the Trail of Tears. The survivors ended up in a place they named Tahlequah. Today Tahlequah is a modern city with street signs in Cherokee.

"Tsa-la-gi s hi-wo-ni?" (Do you speak Cherokee?) At one time, it was illegal for American Indian people to speak their own languages. Today teams of kids compete in the Cherokee Language Bowl, which helps keep that language alive. Members of the Cherokee National Youth Choir sing only in their native language. These seventh to twelfth graders perform all over the United States and at the annual Cherokee National Holiday in Tahlequah.

"¿Habla español?" (Do you speak Spanish?) New students arriving from Spanish-speaking countries like Mexico attend summer programs to learn English, math, and science. Many of their parents migrated to Tahlequah because work was available in its plant nurseries and factories. Cinco de Mayo is a celebration of Mexico's defeat of the invading French on May 5, 1862. Mexicans in Tahlequah honor the day with dancing, food, and an explosion of lively music performed by mariachi bands.

"Parlez-vous français?" (Do you speak French?) Tahlequah kids don't have to travel far to hear French. The city holds its own mini Mardi Gras celebration, like the famous one in New Orleans, Louisiana. A children's carnival, a parade, crawdads to eat, and spectacular floats add to the fun. Everyone goes home with lots of toys and trinkets. Tahlequah's rich mix of cultures and languages makes it a lively, colorful place to live.

Playground fun in Tahlequah

Going for a touchdown

## More about
# Tahlequah

**Founded:** 1843

**Total population:** 14,458

**Youth population:** 4,265

**Nickname:** Best Small Town in Oklahoma

**Some languages heard in Tahlequah:** Cherokee, Chinese, French, Hindi, Spanish

**Sister city:** None

OKLAHOMA

# PORTLAND

Getting to know the city's top-notch public transit system

Portlanders think living here is all roses

Mount Hood provides a majestic backdrop for the city of Portland, Oregon. Plenty of rain (it rains 150 days a year!) keeps Portland's plants lush and green. The city boasts over two hundred parks, including Forest Park, the largest wilderness park located within city limits in the United States. Kids can hike, bike, and ride horses in its more than five thousand acres. Portland may also have the world's smallest park. Mill Ends Park, twenty-four inches in diameter, is so little you can barely stand in it. Since the park was created in 1948, people have added things to it, like rose plants and a diving board for butterflies.

Kids can also stop and smell the roses in Portland's many gardens. Portland is called the City of Roses, and its largest public rose garden has more than eight thousand bushes. The Castilian rose, famous for its fragrance, was brought to Portland from Mexico in 1830. You can still see it in Portland's gardens today. Perhaps some vaqueros (cowboys) brought these fragrant flowers with them when they came to Oregon to herd cattle.

In the 1870s Chinese began migrating to Portland from California and Asia. More than a hundred years later, Chinese American landscape designers built a classical Chinese garden that takes up a full city block in downtown Portland. The garden is modeled after ancient gardens in the Chinese city of Suzhou, Portland's sister city. Winding stone paths lead visitors to rare flowers and surprising views of plants and trees.

Japanese immigrants, many of whom came to Portland in the late 1870s, also had a way with plants. They created calm and peaceful gardens based on traditional designs. Many Japanese gardens feature beautiful ponds filled with

Cool off with an ice-cold drink at Ricky's stand!

Portland has a large
Asian American population

brightly colored koi fish. On Children's Day, a traditional Japanese holiday, kids can drink tea, paint with black *sumi-e* ink, and watch the koi swim. Today many yards and parks throughout the city display moss-covered rock gardens based on the Japanese style.

## More about
# Portland

**Founded:** 1845

**Total population:** 529,121

**Youth population:** 125,561

**Nickname:** City of Roses

**Some languages heard in Portland:** Chinese, Haitian Creole, Japanese, Somali, Spanish

**Sister cities:** Sapporo, Japan; Suzhou, China

# LANCASTER

Riding in an Amish horse-drawn buggy

Wearing a stole in honor of Holy Week

**D**id you know that Lancaster was the capital of the United States for a single day? On September 19, 1777, the new American government retreated from the original capital, Philadelphia, to escape British troops. The new Congress stayed in Lancaster for one day. Snuggled along the Susquehanna River in southeastern Pennsylvania, Lancaster is an important part of U.S. history. It was once the largest inland city in the country.

Farmers have been selling produce in Central Market, the oldest farmers' market in the United States, since 1750. Little has changed, including the way that farmers get to the market. Many still come by horse and wagon! The bustling city of Lancaster is located in the center of an Amish farming community. The Amish are a Christian group that chooses to live simply.

Most Amish people do not use cars, telephones, or electricity, or wear bright clothing. They believe humility, family, and community bring them closer to God, and they find this easier to achieve by staying separated from the modern world. Amish children attend one-room schools until the eighth grade. Many then choose to work on the family farm instead of going to high school. Most

Amish children speak three languages: English, German, and a German dialect called Pennsylvania Dutch. They make their own clothing and raise their own food right outside the city limits. The Amish are famous for their barn raisings, during which the entire community builds a barn together.

In 2000 Lancaster was recognized as an All-America City, an honor awarded to communities whose citizens work together to solve problems creatively. Community groups turned a vacant lot into a park and started a charter school to keep kids from dropping out.

The dance group *Huellas Latinos* (Latin Footsteps) helps kids stay in school, too. Before Puerto Rican and Dominican kids can salsa or toprock across the stage, they have to boogie through their books, earning high grades. The dance program's director teaches kids the merengue and hip-hop and helps them with homework. In keeping with Latino customs, the group even has an *abuelita* (little grandma) who helps kids solve their problems.

A chess champ captures another piece

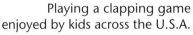

Playing a clapping game enjoyed by kids across the U.S.A.

## More about
# Lancaster

**Founded:** 1742

**Total population:** 56,348

**Youth population:** 17,793

**Nickname:** Red Rose City

**Some languages heard in Lancaster:**
German, Pennsylvania Dutch, Russian, Spanish, Vietnamese

**Sister city:** None

# PROVIDENCE

Sharing Hmong culture in Providence

Meeting a turtle at the
Providence Children's Museum

In 1635 Roger Williams was banished from the Puritan Massachusetts Bay Colony because he believed that people should be free to worship in their own way, and that religion should be separate from government. Williams wanted to build a city that would be fair and diverse. He founded Providence on land given to him by the Narragansetts. Today, residents of all backgrounds, including the Narragansetts, try to stay true to this dream of a friendly, welcoming city.

Holi, the Hindu Festival of Colors, is a time to forgive and make new friends. During this northern Indian holiday, Providence kids splash colored powder on each other to represent the colors of spring. Indian American kids and their friends wind up with red and yellow faces and hands.

Imagine using your hands, instead of your voice, to speak with your friends! At the Rhode Island School for the Deaf, kids communicate in American Sign Language. Not only can they sign up a storm, they also have championship basketball and track teams. The young athletes and their classmates study math, science, and history, all in sign language.

Providence kids can learn about the history of Armenian Americans, who have enriched the life of the city for over a century. Many Armenians came as war orphans in the late 1800s, fleeing from fighting that killed tens of thousands of people in Asia Minor. Armenian churches became the heart of their new community. Kids still study Armenian, learn to cook *gatah* (sweet rolls), and hear Armenian folk stories in the churches. One funny tale is about a man who is afraid of everything but ends up being called Nazar the Brave.

The Roger Williams Park Zoo has more than 1,000 animals!

Lithuanian American kids anxiously wait for the first star to appear during Kucious, an ancient winter solstice ritual that has become a Christmas Eve celebration. Then they enjoy a feast of meatless dishes like *kugelis* (baked potato pudding) and share in the eating of an apple to represent joy. Their ancestors from Lithuania, a small country in eastern Europe, often faced severe hardships and injustices. But they found safety and happiness in Providence, whose motto is "What cheer!"

Singing is a great way to practice reading

Dressed in a traditional Armenian outfit for a dance recital

## More about
# Providence

**Founded:** 1636

**Total population:** 173,618

**Youth population:** 56,317

**Nickname:** Beehive of Industry

**Some languages used in Providence:** American Sign Language, Armenian, Hindi, Hmong, Lithuanian

**Sister city:** Santo Domingo, Dominican Republic

RHODE ISLAND

# CHARLESTON

Charleston kids have plenty of coastline to explore

**"T**engk' Gawd fuh Chaa'stun" is what you might hear if you talk to a Gullah resident of Charleston. It means "Thank God for Charleston" in the Gullah language, which has links to the English of Shakespeare's day and to the languages of Sierra Leone, Angola, and Barbados. The Gullah language may have been developed so that people who were brought here from different countries as slaves could talk to each other. Authors Virginia Mixson Geraty and Robert San Souci write exciting Gullah stories for all kids.

Gullah children are part of a culture unlike any other in the world. They can trace their roots to the first Africans arriving in Charleston's low country in the early 1600s. This low-lying area of land sits next to the ocean. It includes tidal flats, marshes, beaches, and islands. Older family members teach children traditional arts like net making and weaving baskets out of sweetgrass found in the marshes.

African American history is important to South Carolina's kids

In the eighteenth century African and African American slaves were forced to use their agricultural knowledge to convert South Carolina swamps into rice fields. Caw Caw Interpretive Center is built on a former plantation near Charleston. Kids can walk through the historic rice fields and learn how men, women, and children labored to plant and harvest the famous Carolina rice. They can also enjoy listening to Gullah music and storytelling.

Kids can learn about a different culture at the annual Scottish Games and Highland Gathering. It is a time to enjoy bagpipe music and dance the Highland fling. Kids and adults play traditional Scottish games like the hammer throw and the caber toss. In the adults' version of the caber toss, contestants toss a caber,

Chow down! Crayfish are
a real Charleston treat

a 130-pound log that is about the length of a telephone
pole. In the kids' version of the game, children toss a
hollow cardboard log.

With so much going on in Charleston, even some dead
residents want to join the fun! Charleston is famous for
ghosts like the Headless Torso of the Battery Carriage
House and the Gullah Boo Hag, a bloodred creature with
no skin. Visitors can stay at haunted inns, if they dare!

Music of all kinds fills
the air in Charleston

## More about
# Charleston

**Founded:** 1670

**Total population:** 96,650

**Youth population:** 24,642

**Nickname:** The Holy City

**Some languages heard in Charleston:**
Chinese, Gullah, Hindi, Korean,
Scottish Gaelic

**Sister city:** Spoleto, Italy

# RAPID CITY

A young cowboy practices roping

A brontosaurus and a tyrannosaurus stand guard over Rapid City, South Dakota, from their spots in Dinosaur Park. These concrete giants are right at home in the foothills of the Black Hills, an area loaded with fossils of real prehistoric animals. Girls from Operation SMART get a chance to study both dinosaur relics and live animals firsthand. They have fun blending math, science, and technology as they examine fossils, learn about farm animals, and explore the habitats of wolves, bears, and mountain lions.

The Black Hills around Rapid City are named for their pine forests, which are so thick they look black. The hills are sacred to the Lakotas, who call them Paha Sapa. These American Indians believe that the hills were set aside for birds and animals and that people should not live there. When gold was discovered in the 1800s, miners rushed in, and Rapid City sprang up. Today Lakota people still strive for the safe return of the sacred hills. At the Lakota Nation Invitational, Lakota and non-Lakota kids compete in boxing, basketball, and wrestling.

Performing a Lakota dance

Nearby at Ellsworth Air Force Base, kids from all over the country are stationed with their parents. Living on a military base is like being in a separate city, complete with stores, houses, schools, and places of worship. Kids from Ellsworth join other Rapid City kids in the Pennington County 4-H program. They gain skills in caring for horses, cows, rabbits, dogs, and other animals. They can learn about each other's cultures, too, as they prepare their animals for the fairs. A favorite event is the dog agility competition, in which dogs twist, turn, and jump to complete an obstacle course.

Dogs are also a main attraction at the Dakota Celtic Festival and Highland Games. Thousands of people gather to watch border collies skillfully herding sheep. Over one hundred years ago, immigrants brought these and other hardworking dogs all the way from Ireland and Scotland to Rapid City. From dinosaurs to horses to dogs, today's Rapid City kids have lots of chances to learn about animals up close.

Learning about Lakota culture from an elder

Kids care for animals
(and more!) through 4-H

You can still hang out with a
brontosaurus in the Black Hills

## More about
## Rapid City

**Founded:** 1876

**Total population:** 59,607

**Youth population:** 17,105

**Nickname:** Shining Star of the West

**Some languages heard in Rapid City:** German, Korean, Lakota, Spanish, Tagalog

**Sister cities:** Apolda, Germany; Imaichi, Japan

97

# NASHVILLE

Learning to pick, bend, and strum in Music City

Beautiful in traditional Laotian
jewelry and handwoven silk

The Grand Ole Opry, the world center of country music, is right in the center of Nashville, the capital of Tennessee. Celebrated performers like LeAnn Rimes, Dolly Parton, and the late Johnny Cash have performed on its huge stage.

Stars of all sorts light up this town. Nashville draws many outstanding shows and exhibits, such as "Manuel: Star-Spangled Couture." In this traveling display, fifty brightly embroidered jackets show each state's character and history. Mexican-born Manuel created these jackets to honor the United States. The famous designer has also made spectacular costumes for Elvis Presley, the members of the rock band Aerosmith, and many other stars.

Across town, outfits of shimmering blues, reds, golds, and purples light up the Boon Pee Mai (Laotian New Year) festivities. The Royal Lao Classical Children Dancers wear glorious costumes when they perform for Buddhist holiday celebrations. At the Buddhapathip Temple, kids learn the Laotian language and traditions like respecting and caring for everyone in the community.

Dazzling fireworks explode over the white towers of Nashville's Sri Ganisha Hindu Temple during Diwali, the Festival of Lights. Nashville has about eight thousand Indian American families, and many Hindus, Sikhs, Jains, and members of other religions celebrate Diwali to welcome the New Year. Kids usually get new clothes for the holiday. Boys wear spiffy slacks and shirts, while girls wear vibrant *salwar kameezay* (tunics with pants).

On special occasions Kurdish girls wear *sarmil* (traditional dresses) with *krasas* (pants) in rainbow hues. Nashville has the largest community of Kurds in the country. Some gatherings feature the bright yellow sun and red, white, and green stripes of the Kurdish flag.

The world's largest Earth Day flag was made by kids from around the world who expressed their feelings about the environment by drawing on individual squares of material. The squares were sewn together by Nashville-based Kids for a Clean Environment (Kids F.A.C.E.), started by Melissa Poe when she was only nine. The finished flag is twice the size of a basketball court! Kids F.A.C.E., which now has members from twenty-three countries, is an organization for kids who want to grow up in a pollution-free world.

**TENNESSEE**

Performing at a dance recital

## More about
## Nashville

**Founded:** 1779

**Total population:** 545,524

**Youth population:** 138,865

**Nicknames:** Athens of the South; Music City, U.S.A.

**Some languages heard in Nashville:** Hindi, Kurdish, Laotian, Nuer, Spanish

**Sister cities:** Belfast, Ireland; Edmonton, Canada

Nashville kids of all backgrounds chase the world and all that's in it!

# HOUSTON

Houston's skyline rises behind a downtown park

"Houston" was the first word astronaut Neil Armstrong spoke as he became the first person to walk on the moon on July 20, 1969. Houston is mission control headquarters for manned U.S. space flights. Houston does everything in a BIG way! It's the largest city in the South and the nation's fourth largest in population. The city is home to more than one hundred ethnic groups. Over ninety languages are spoken in Houston homes.

Every year Houstonians celebrate the city's diversity with a huge international festival. The festival spotlights a different country each year. In 2004 the festival captured the sights and sounds of Thailand. Some kids got their pictures taken with five trained Asian elephants! These intelligent animals are the national symbol of Thailand.

Houston also hosts the three-week-long Livestock Show and Rodeo. Kids from eight to nineteen years old show their cattle, sheep, horses, and rabbits and sell them to the highest bidders. If kids prefer painting and sculpting to raising livestock, they can submit original art projects with western themes. The rodeo event raises millions of dollars for Texas youth.

The word *rodeo* comes from the Spanish *rodear*, meaning "to go round," as in rounding up cattle. *Charro* (Mexican cowboy) exhibitions were popular in Texas long before white settlers arrived. *Charros* showed off their horsemanship, roped calves, and rode bulls. In 1993 Houston rodeo organizers reached out to the city's large Mexican community. Now mariachi bands stroll the grounds on Go Tejano Day, which celebrates Mexican influences on the rodeo.

The rodeo organizers also formed the Black Go Texan Committee. Committee members raise money for scholarships and spotlight black history in Texas and

Explore, learn, and goof off at the Children's Museum

A Texas teen gives it
her all at the rodeo

the West. During slavery many blacks in Texas tended horses and cattle on ranches. On June 19, 1865, Texas slaves finally learned they were free, or emancipated. Today African Americans make up a quarter of Houston's population. They celebrate a holiday called Juneteenth that honors the June emancipation date. For an entire month, Houstonians are treated to blues, gospel, jazz, and other events. Juneteenth is a big festival in a city that truly does it up BIG.

Welcome to Space City, U.S.A.—
America's gateway to the universe!

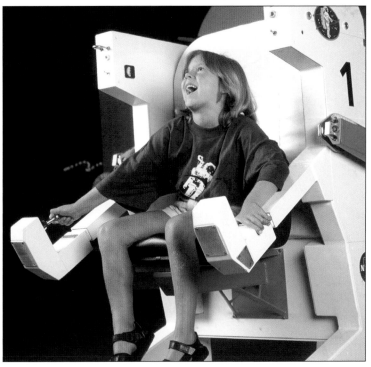

## More about
# Houston

**Founded:** 1836

**Total population:** 1,953,631

**Youth population:** 593,888

**Nicknames:** Space City, Energy Capital
  of the World

**Some languages heard in Houston:**
  Filipino, Greek, Spanish, Thai, Turkish

**Sister cities:** Abu Dhabi, United Arab
  Emirates; Luanda, Angola

# SALT LAKE CITY

A snowboarder hammers down a slope of the Wasatch Mountains

**H**iking, biking, skiing, and snowboarding are just a few of the things kids love to do in the Wasatch Range. These mountains welcomed world-class athletes when Salt Lake City was home to the 2002 Winter Olympics. In the snowcapped peaks, skiers can hit the slopes well into the spring.

For centuries Utes in the Salt Lake City area have celebrated spring with a bear dance. The dance music imitates the bears' raspy growls after winter hibernation. This public festival honors nature's power and the season of new beginnings. For several days American Indians and others dance, feast, and play games.

In 1847 Mormon leader Brigham Young and other Mormon pioneers made a dangerous trek from Illinois to the Salt Lake Valley. They were fleeing eastern towns where mobs attacked them because of their religious beliefs. The Mormon settlers planted crops and began putting down roots.

By 1870 Salt Lake City's population was mostly Mormon. Traveling Mormon missionaries convinced Scandinavians and Pacific Islanders to bring their families and skills to the city. Today the six-spired granite Mormon Temple stands in Temple Square. This center of the Church of Jesus Christ of Latter-day Saints, the formal name for the Mormon faith, took forty years to build.

Salt Lake City is home to people of many faiths. The city's Buddhist temple was built by descendants of the Japanese

Buddhists who helped build the city's first railroads. They observe Shusho-E (Grand Prayer Ceremony) on New Year's Day to renew their faith. Muslims from Pakistan, Egypt, and Iran pray at the Islamic center and observe the holy month of Ramadan, a time for charity and fellowship. At Congregation Kol Ami, Jewish boys and girls are honored in the bar and bat mitzvah coming-of-age ceremonies.

Salt Lake City is also the location of Brigham Young University, founded by the Mormons. Education in this state capital has a silly side as well as a serious one. An elementary-school principal promised that if students read for three hundred thousand minutes, she would kiss a pig. The kids reached the goal, and the principal kissed a pig in front of the entire school!

Celebrating Pioneer Day, a Utah holiday honoring the Mormon pioneers

Getting an affectionate nuzzle from a therapy dog

Planting trees to care for the environment

## More about
## Salt Lake City

**Founded:** 1847

**Total population:** 181,743

**Youth population:** 49,262

**Nickname:** Crossroads of the West

**Some languages heard in Salt Lake City:**
Japanese, Swedish, Tahitian, Urdu, Ute

**Sister cities:** Chernivtsi, Ukraine; Quezon City, Philippines

UTAH

# BURLINGTON

Somali Bantu traditions come to Vermont

Every winter, Burlington gets over six feet of snow!

A forty-foot-long creature with a horse-shaped head is said to live in Lake Champlain near Burlington, Vermont. Some think it may be a plesiosaur, a kind of dinosaur, that survived extinction! No one knows for sure if it really exists, but the Vermont government placed this creature, nicknamed Champ, on the endangered species list.

The first people to report seeing Champ were Abenaki Indians. Their home was in the area's majestic Green Mountains. Fierce conflicts arose between the Abenaki and early European colonists, but the Abenaki survived. Their descendants have been joined in the Burlington area by people from around the world.

Many of the more recent newcomers arrived after fleeing ethnic violence in their homelands. A group of young men from Sudan, in East Africa, found refuge in Burlington after a legendary escape from their country's long civil war. As children, they walked hundreds of miles through rain forests and across deserts, helping each other to safety. In Burlington they go to school and help each other with their lessons. Many dream of returning to Sudan to share their newfound skills.

Tibetan families came to Burlington from their refuge in India. Many fled Tibet when the Chinese occupied their homeland. Although Vermont's Green Mountains are not nearly as high as Tibet's towering Himalayas, they help Tibetans feel at home.

Bosnian kids from eastern Europe, who lived through a brutal war, now have a peaceful home in the city. The Bosnian Lilies, a children's dance troupe, performs Bosnian folk dances. Girls decked out in red, pink, or green satin and boys dressed in black with red cummerbunds kick up their heels to centuries-old songs.

A peaceful world is on the menu along with Chunky Monkey and Cherry Garcia ice cream at

At the Intervale Center's "Healthy City," young entrepreneurs learn how to run an organic farm

Ben and Jerry's. Company founders and former owners Ben Cohen and Jerry Greenfield used their profits to actively protect the environment and promote peace. At the company's Burlington headquarters you can learn fifty ways to work for peace at home and in the world as you enjoy a scoop of your favorite ice cream.

Trading a wheelchair for a soap box racer

Ben & Jerry's ice cream is a favorite Burlington treat

## More about
## Burlington

**Founded:** 1773

**Total population:** 38,889

**Youth population:** 8,870

**Some languages heard in Burlington:** Albanian, Bosnian, Dinka, Romani, Tibetan

**Sister cities:** Bethlehem, Palestinian Authority; Puerto Cabezas, Nicaragua

# RICHMOND

Students enjoy a special school assembly

At the Asian Festival, kids learn how to use a Chinese yoyo

Richmond, Virginia's capital city, proves change is possible. It was the capital of the Confederacy in 1861 and a whites-only city for many years after the Civil War. Slowly African Americans established themselves there. Their work helped change many public attitudes. In 1977 Richmond elected its first black mayor. In 1990 Lawrence Douglas Wilder, the grandson of slaves, became the nation's first elected African American governor.

In 1903 Maggie Lena Walker, the daughter of slaves, started a bank in Richmond's Jackson Ward, the largest black business district in the South. She was the country's first woman bank founder and president. Many African Americans opened savings accounts in which they deposited a penny or nickel a week. Walker's bank helped hundreds of people buy homes. The bank still operates today.

Arthur Ashe, a champion tennis player, was born in Richmond. As a teen, he had to compete in out-of-state matches because Virginia wouldn't allow African Americans to play on local courts. In 1975 he was named the world's number one player. Before Ashe died in 1993 of AIDS, which he contracted through a blood transfusion, he devoted himself to finding a cure for the disease. In 1996 Richmond honored him with a statue on Monument Avenue.

Richmond is home to the Virginia Baptist Historical Society. Ever since Baptists began establishing churches in Virginia in the 1700s, they have helped shape Richmond and the United States. Before the American Revolution, they sought freedom from the restrictions of the Church of England. Their struggle influenced James Madison and other founding fathers to include protection for religious freedom in the Bill of Rights. Thanks to the First Amendment, kids and their families are free to worship as they choose.

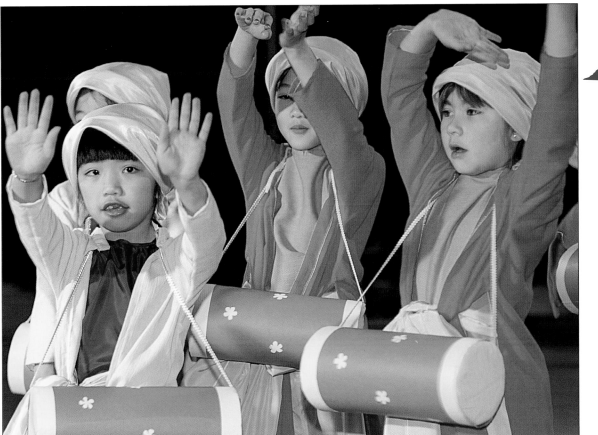

Performing a traditional Vietnamese Drum Dance

Many members of Richmond's Latino community are Catholic, and some churches offer Mass in Spanish. People from Pakistan, Iran, and Lebanon are part of the city's growing Muslim community. The Richmond city council reflects change, too. The customary prayer before each council meeting has been offered by Muslim, Christian, and Jewish spiritual leaders.

The Richmond Bluegrass Festival is full of banjos, barn dances, and bandanas

## More about
# Richmond

**Founded:** 1682

**Total population:** 197,790

**Youth population:** 50,724

**Some languages heard in Richmond:** Arabic, French, Korean, Spanish, Tagalog

**Sister cities:** Uijongbu, South Korea; Windhoek, Namibia

# SEATTLE

Home of Microsoft, Seattle is a city of techies!

Visitors love to get their hands wet at the aquarium

From Seattle's famous Space Needle tower, you can see the waters of Puget Sound and the snowcapped peak of Mount Rainier. Named for Chief Seal'th of the Duwamish nation, Seattle is rich with American Indian traditions. Seafair, Seattle's most famous festival, was called Potlatch until 1950. A potlatch is an elaborate ceremony held among American Indians from the Northwest Coast.

Seafair has become an intercultural festival. The International District, a predominantly Asian neighborhood, invites festival goers to experience cultures that originated on the other side of the Pacific Ocean. Guided by Japanese artists, visitors can try their hands at *origami* (paper folding) and *kirigami* (paper cutting).

Seattle's information technology (IT) industry draws people from Asia and around the world. Microsoft, headquartered in nearby Redmond, has employees from over 135 countries. Area IT professionals mentor kids, giving some their first exposure to computers and motivating them to excel in school and in life.

Asian Americans have long made Seattle their home, but they have not always been welcomed as neighbors. In the nineteenth century some white laborers, fearing that Chinese settlers would take away their jobs, started anti-Chinese riots. During World War II the U.S. government suspected that people of Japanese descent might be spies for Japan. All Japanese Americans in the Northwest, even those who had been Americans for generations, were forced to live in internment camps. The U.S. government officially apologized to the Japanese American community in 1988. Despite these hardships Asians have found success in Seattle. Gary Locke became Washington's governor in 1996, making him the first Chinese American governor in the country. A Japanese American architect, Minoru Yamasaki, designed New York's World Trade Center. Both were born in Seattle.

Seattle's many cultures connect kids around the globe

Carrying groceries from Seattle's outdoor markets

Seattle is also home to a vibrant Scandinavian culture. Tens of thousands of Swedes, Norwegians, and Finns began to settle in Seattle in the 1880s. Every May one of the largest ethnic parades in the United States takes place there to celebrate Norwegian Constitution Day. Norwegian Americans wear *bunader* (folk costumes), and everyone eats a hearty lunch of codfish, potatoes, cauliflower, and almond cake.

## More about
# Seattle

**Founded:** 1852

**Total population:** 563,374

**Youth population:** 103,747

**Nickname:** Emerald City

**Some languages heard in Seattle:** Cambodian, Chinese, Japanese, Ladino, Norwegian

**Sister cities:** Bergen, Norway; Surabaya, Indonesia

# WHEELING

Dancers show off their fancy footwork at the Wheeling Celtic Festival

The craft fair at Wheeling's African American Jubilee attracts all ages

The huge Grave Creek Mound rises seven stories into the sky outside Wheeling, West Virginia. A group of American Indians called the Adenas built this burial mound over three thousand years ago. No one knows what happened to them or how they erected this masterpiece centuries before there were bulldozers or cranes. Based on objects found at the site, archaeologists know that the Adenas traveled far, trading with other American Indian peoples from the Great Lakes to the Gulf of Mexico.

Travelers continued to come through Wheeling. In the 1800s Wheeling was a stopover town for frontiersmen and homesteaders heading west on the first National Road. Snaking through the town, the National Road crossed over the Wheeling Suspension Bridge, the first bridge over the Ohio River. Not far from the National Road sits the Kruger Street Toy and Train Museum. Visitors can climb aboard a restored caboose for a pretend trip around the city.

Not all travelers crossed the river and continued west. As more and more industry moved into the area, people had reasons to stay. Many African Americans escaping slavery on the Underground Railroad settled down in this proud, free city. Each June Wheeling is home to the fun-filled African American Jubilee, which showcases black music, art, and history.

European immigrants were first attracted to jobs in Wheeling's steel mills in the 1850s. The Italian American influence on the city is celebrated each July when Wheeling becomes Little Italy. Kids love to chow down on "little worms," English for *vermicelli* pasta! The spirit and strength of Wheeling's Irish American community are proudly displayed during the Wheeling Celtic Festival. And the Temple Shalom museum tells the story of how Jews settled in the city.

Lebanese and Syrian immigrants also started arriving in the late nineteenth century. Now every August Our Lady of Lebanon Church hosts its annual *mahrajan* (festival) on the Feast of the *Sa-idy* (Assumption). Neighbors and friends from far away join in the *dubki*, a traditional Lebanese dance, holding hands and dancing in a big circle. Mouthwatering Lebanese goodies like *kibbee*, a dish made with ground lamb; *shish kebab*; and stuffed grape leaves are served up along with games and music.

At the Challenger Learning Center

Teens perform a dance at the *mahrajan*

Budding musicians in the Wheeling Symphony Youth Orchestra

## More about
# Wheeling

**Founded:** 1793

**Total population:** 31,419

**Youth population:** 7,394

**Nickname:** Friendly City

**Some languages heard in Wheeling:** Arabic, Greek, Hindi, Italian, Spanish

**Sister City:** None

# WEST VIRGINIA

# MILWAUKEE

A young *fraülein* celebrates German Fest

Kids love Lake Michigan's beaches

**M**ilwaukee is an Algonquian word meaning "gathering place by the waters." Long ago the Sauk, Fox, Ojibwa, Odawa, and Potawatomi Algonquian nations held get-togethers in the area. Today Milwaukee is still true to its name. Immigrants from nations around the world have gathered in this port city on Lake Michigan and called it home.

Many German immigrants settled in Milwaukee, Wisconsin's largest city. By the 1850s they made up almost half the city's population. They lived in *Kleindeutschlands* (little Germanys) where they spoke German, built German-style houses, read German newspapers, and ran kindergartens. They gathered together to sing, compete in sports, and socialize in the city's beer gardens and bowling clubs. Today Milwaukee has over two thousand bowling alleys! One alley welcomes young children by providing lightweight balls and bumpers that keep kids from throwing only gutter balls.

Milwaukee is called the City of Festivals. Every summer during the three-day German Fest at the Maier Festival Park, people from all over the city gather to have a good time. In the children's area, Pretzel Park, kids can twist dough into pretzels or play German-language bingo. When they aren't practicing polka dance steps or marching in the children's fairy-tale parade, kids can snack on mouthwatering foods like frankfurters (hot dogs) covered with sauerkraut (cabbage) and mustard, which is a German favorite. One year thirty-eight Milwaukee German clubs cooked up ten thousand pounds of potato pancakes and more than ten thousand pounds of sauerkraut during the festival.

Large numbers of Polish immigrants have also gathered in Milwaukee. They make up the second-largest ethnic group in

Painting flags at the Asian Moon Fest

the city. Polish groceries and restaurants on the city's south side offer dill pickle soup and pierogies (pan-fried dumplings filled with cheese, vegetables, or meat). *Wycinanki* (VEE-chee-non-key) artists teach kids the intricate art of Polish paper cutting. The artists fold paper over and over and then cut off pieces from the corners. When they open up the paper, they reveal snowflake-like cuttings of people, flowers, animals, and whole scenes.

Roller coaster fun at Summer Fest

Frilly skirts at a Mexican fiesta

## More about
# Milwaukee

**Founded:** 1836

**Total population:** 596,974

**Youth population:** 192,019

**Nicknames:** Cream City, City of Festivals

**Some languages heard in Milwaukee:** German, Hmong, Italian, Polish, Spanish

**Sister cities:** Bialystok, Poland; King Williams Town, South Africa

113

# CHEYENNE

The tough Wyoming winter gets balanced
by summer days in the 90s

This young cowgirl loves the rodeo!

**M**r. T twisted, jumped, kicked high in the air, and threw his 188th cowboy. This rodeo bull worked hard for his spot as one of Cheyenne's most famous residents. Finally, in 1989 cowboy Marty Staneart stayed on Mr. T for eight seconds, ending the bull's winning streak.

Cheyenne, Wyoming's capital, is perched on the high plains in the southeast corner of the state. It started as a railroad community, full of rootin'-tootin' cowboys in town for cattle drives. Both residents and visitors lived a rough-and-tumble life. Women had to be tough to survive in Cheyenne, so it is no surprise that Cheyenne's women were the first in the United States to win the right to vote.

Today cowboy culture lives on during Cheyenne Frontier Days. Food, music, and demonstrations show what it was like to live in a western town. Rodeo athletes, including American Indian cowboys and cowgirls, come from all over to compete in one of the world's largest rodeos. The festival's Indian Village features the cultures of the Arapahos and Shoshones, many of whom live on the nearby Wind River Reservation. Sacagawea, the Shoshone

Special Friends Aviation Club
members about to take flight

guide for the Lewis and Clark expedition, is buried there.

American Indian students attend Cheyenne schools with kids from countries as far away as Croatia, Korea, and Puerto Rico. Some children help their homelands by taking part in the Empty Bowls project. They make ceramic bowls and serve meals in them to guests. The guests donate money to organizations fighting hunger.

Cheyenne kids make a difference in lots of ways. Many of them helped build the award-winning Greenway, a fourteen-mile path around Cheyenne where they can bike, skate, jog, or cruise in wheelchairs. They and lots of other volunteers also helped build benches and picnic tables and plant trees and shrubs along the path. Working together, these environmentalists keep the trail clean and beautiful for all of Cheyenne's residents and visitors to enjoy.

Training in the Arapaho art of archery

## More about
# Cheyenne

**Founded:** 1867

**Total population:** 53,011

**Youth population:** 14,537

**Nickname:** Magic City of the Plains

**Some languages heard in Cheyenne:** Arapaho, Croatian, Greek, Korean, Shoshone

**Sister cities:** Lourdes, France; Taichung, Taiwan

115

# RESOURCES

## Books for Children

Altman, Linda Jacobs. *Amelia's Road.* Illustrated by Enrique O. Sanchez. New York: Lee & Low Books, 1993.

Buller, Laura. *A Faith Like Mine: A Celebration of the World's Religions Through the Eyes of Children.* New York: Dorling Kindersley, 2005.

Cohn, Janice. *The Christmas Menorahs: How a Town Fought Hate.* Illustrated by Bill Farnsworth. Morton Grove, IL: Albert Whitman, 1995.

Cook, Deanna F. *The Kids' Multicultural Cookbook: Food and Fun Around the World.* Illustrated by Michael P. Kline. Nashville, TN: Williamson Publishing, 1995.

Cushman, Karen. *Rodzina.* New York: Clarion Books, 2003.

Dennis, Yvonne Wakim, and Arlene Hirschfelder. *Children of Native America Today.* Watertown, MA: Charlesbridge, 2003.

Friedman, Ina R. *How My Parents Learned to Eat.* Illustrated by Allen Say. Boston: Houghton Mifflin, 1984.

Garza, Carmen Lomas. *Family Pictures/Cuadros de Familia.* 15th anniversary edition. San Francisco: Children's Book Press, 2005.

Hamilton, Virginia. *Her Stories: African American Folktales, Fairy Tales, and True Tales.* Illustrated by Leo and Diane Dillon. New York: Blue Sky Press, 1995.

Hoose, Phillip M. *We Were There, Too! Young People in U.S. History.* New York: Farrar, Straus & Giroux, 2001.

Hopkins, Lee Bennett, ed. *My America: A Poetry Atlas of the United States.* Illustrated by Stephen Alcorn. New York: Simon & Schuster, 2000.

Kirk, Connie Ann. *Sky Dancers.* Illustrated by Christy Hale. New York: Lee & Low Books, 2004.

Krishnaswami, Uma. *Chachaji's Cup.* Illustrated by Soumya Sitaraman. San Francisco: Children's Book Press, 2003.

Kuklin, Susan. *How My Family Lives in America.* New York: Simon & Schuster, 1992.

Larson, Kirby. *Hattie Big Sky.* New York: Delacorte, 2006.

Lawlor, Veronica, ed. *I Was Dreaming to Come to America: Memories from the Ellis Island Oral History Project.* Reprint. New York: Puffin, 1997.

Leacock, Elspeth, and Susan Buckley. *Journeys in Time: A New Atlas of American History.* Illustrated by Rodica Prato. Boston: Houghton Mifflin, 2001.

Lester, Julius. *Let's Talk About Race.* Illustrated by Karen Barbour. New York: HarperCollins, 2005.

McKay, Lawrence, Jr. *Journey Home.* Illustrated by Dom Lee and Keunhee Lee. New York: Lee & Low Books, 1998.

McWhorter, Diane. *A Dream of Freedom: The Civil Rights Movement from 1954 to 1968.* New York: Scholastic, 2004.

Mitchell, Lori. *Different Just Like Me.* Watertown, MA: Charlesbridge, 1999.

Myers, Walter Dean. *Jazz.* Illustrated by Christopher Myers. New York: Holiday House, 2006.

Na, An. *A Step from Heaven*. Asheville, NC: Front Street, 2001.

Nye, Naomi Shihab. *Sitti's Secrets*. Illustrated by Nancy Carpenter. Reprint. New York: Aladdin, 1997.

Osborne, Mary Pope. *One World, Many Religions: The Ways We Worship*. New York: Knopf, 1996.

Robb, Don. *This Is America: The American Spirit in Places and People*. Illustrated by Christine Joy Pratt. Watertown, MA: Charlesbridge, 2005.

Smith, Charles R., Jr. *I Am America*. New York: Scholastic, 2003.

Winter, Jonah. *¡Béisbol! Latino Baseball Pioneers and Legends*. New York: Lee & Low Books, 2001.

Woodruff, Elvira. *The Memory Coat*. Illustrated by Michael Dooling. New York: Scholastic, 1999.

## Book Series for Kids

American Girls Collection. Middleton, WI: Pleasant Company Publications.

Hoobler, Dorothy, and Thomas Hoobler. The American Family Albums. New York: Oxford University Press.

My Name Is America. New York: Scholastic.

Nixon, Joan Lowery. Ellis Island. New York: Bantam Doubleday Dell.

## Magazines for Kids

*Appleseeds*. Explores global history and culture.

*Cobblestone*. Articles and activities on American history.

*Footsteps*. Celebrates African American history, heritage, and culture.

*New Moon*. Created by and for girls.

*Skipping Stones*. Encourages cooperation, creativity, and celebration of cultural and environmental richness.

## Multimedia for Kids

Fink, Cathy, and Marcy Marxer. *Nobody Else Like Me: Celebrating the Diversity of Children*. Cambridge, MA: Rounder Records, 1998. Audio CD.

Fink, Sam. *The Three Documents That Made America: The Declaration of Independence, the Constitution of the U.S.A., and the Bill of Rights*. Middletown, RI: Audio Bookshelf, 2004. Audio CD.

Fleischman, Paul. *Seedfolks*. Middletown, RI: Audio Bookshelf, 2003. Audio CD.

Krull, Kathleen, collector and arranger. *I Hear America Singing! Folk Songs for American Families*. Illustrated by Allen Garns. New York: Alfred A. Knopf, 2003. Book and Audio CD.

Putumayo Kids collection. New York: Putumayo World Music. Audio CDs.

# RESOURCES

## Websites for Kids

American Library Association, "Great Web Sites for Kids"
www.ala.org/parentspage/greatsites

International Children's Digital Library
www.icdlbooks.org

International Kids' Space
www.kids-space.org

KIDPROJ's Multi-Cultural Calendar
www.kidlink.org/KIDPROJ/MCC

The Nifty Fifty States
www.kn.pacbell.com/wired/fil/pages/listthe50sju.html

Peace Corps, Coverdell World Wise Schools
www.peacecorps.gov/wws

United Nations Cyberschoolbus
www.un.org/Pubs/CyberSchoolBus

United Religions Initiative
www.uri.org/kids

## Tools for Parents and Educators

American Folklife Center
www.loc.gov/folklife/index.html

American Library Association, "Multicultural Awards
for Young Readers"
www.ala.org/ala/diversity/versed/versedbackissues/january2005abc/
 multiculturalawards.htm

Angel Island Immigration Station Foundation
www.aiisf.org

Anti-Defamation League, "Education"
www.adl.org/education

Asian American Curriculum Project
www.asianamericanbooks.com

Association of MultiEthnic Americans
www.ameasite.org

Center for Civic Education
www.civiced.org

Center for Research on Education, Diversity and Excellence
http://crede.berkeley.edu

Cross Cultural Health Care Program
www.xculture.org

Denshō: The Japanese American Legacy Project
www.densho.org

Educators for Social Responsibility
www.esrnational.org

Facing History and Ourselves
www.facinghistory.org

Flood, Bo, Beret E. Strong, and William Flood. *Pacific Island Legends: Tales from Micronesia, Melanesia, Polynesia, and Australia.* Illustrated by Connie J. Adams. Honolulu, HI: Bess Press, 1999.

Freedoms Foundation at Valley Forge
www.ffvf.org/over.asp

Hill, Linda D. *Connecting Kids: Exploring Diversity Together.* Gabriola Island, BC, Canada: New Society Publishers, 2001. Activity guide.

Immigration History Research Center
www.ihrc.umn.edu

International Reading Association, "Notable Books for a Global Society"
www.csulb.edu/org/childrens-lit/proj/nbgs/intro-nbgs.html

Kuharets, Olga R., ed. *Venture into Cultures: A Resource Book of Multicultural Materials and Programs.* Chicago: American Library Association, 2001.

National Association for Bilingual Education
www.nabe.org

National Association for Multicultural Education
www.nameorg.org

National Association of School Psychologists, "Cultural Competence"
www.nasponline.org/resources/culturalcompetence/index.aspx

National Council of La Raza
www.nclr.org

National Dissemination Center for Children with Disabilities
www.nichcy.org

National Home Education Network
www.nhen.org

*Native Peoples.* Bimonthly magazine on the arts, culture, and lifeways of Native peoples of the Americas.

*The New York Times* Learning Network
www.nytimes.com/learning/index.html

PBS TeacherSource
www.pbs.org/teachersource

Rand, Donna, and Toni Trent Parker. *Black Books Galore! Guide to More Great African American Children's Books.* New York: Wiley, 2001.

Rethinking Schools Online
www.rethinkingschools.org

Smithsonian Center for Folklife and Cultural Heritage
www.folklife.si.edu/index.html

Special Education Resources on the Internet
www.seriweb.com

Tolerance.org
www.tolerance.org

York, Stacey. *Roots and Wings: Affirming Culture in Early Childhood Programs.* Rev. ed. St. Paul, MN: Redleaf Press, 2003.

RESOURCES

# INDEX

# INDEX (continued)

# ACKNOWLEDGMENTS

Yvonne and Arlene applaud The Global Fund for Children/ Charlesbridge partnership for giving voice to *all* children of the U.S.A. To all the individuals, organizations, and associations that helped us better understand the specialness of your communities, a googolplex of "thank you's" translated into an infinity of languages!

Even more gratitude to Mary Erm for making the little Stroudsburg, Pennsylvania, library a really big place; the Maples Elementary School Arabic Ensemble for amplifying our excitement; the Kurdish Human Rights Watch and Kids F.A.C.E. for making Nashville sparkle; the Montgomery Friendly Supper Club for inviting us to their table; AMISTAD America, Inc., for "sailing" us through history; the Minnesota Humanities Commission for Hmong translations of children's books; the Nevada Historical Society for the reams on Reno; the Hawaiian Portuguese Historical Society and Myung Sa Pai for dancing us across the Pacific; and Virginia Mixson Geraty for *shayayre* (sharing) Gullah traditions.

The long-germinating *Children of the U.S.A.* has relied on the creativity and perseverance of colleagues and the generosity of so many who opened the doors to their homes and communities. The Global Fund for Children thanks the coauthors, the design and editorial team at Charlesbridge, and Kelly Swanson Turner and Magda Nakassis for their indispensable roles. Dean Reuel Jordan and the community of The Bank Street College of Education Children's Programs blessed our project. Their children grace the cover of this book. These, and all the kids who light up the pages of *Children of the U.S.A.*, embody the motto of this nation—"out of many, one."

We thank the helpful folks of the convention and visitors bureaus; city halls; chambers of commerce; newspapers and media; educational, community, and cultural organizations; and families of fifty-one cities across the nation. Besides the photographers and organizations acknowledged on pp. 125–127, we thank Gilroy and Sally Chow, Bridget Daniel, The Delta Blues Museum, The Dilley Family, Grace Housholder, Greater Houston Convention & Visitors Bureau, Joan Lombardi, Janice Randall, and RhodyCo Productions. We are grateful to all who contributed images and their wisdom to this book.

Special thanks to the following educators, who helped gather the children's quotes appearing on pages 8–11.

Adrienne Alinder, Enchanted Hills Elementary School, Rio Rancho, New Mexico; Harriet Allen and Linda Brasel, Sherard Elementary School, Clarksdale, Mississippi; Renee DeTolla, Grand Ridge Elementary School, Issaquah, Washington; Carmen Nakassis, Tilden Middle School, Rockville, Maryland; Catherine Prowse, Maples Elementary School, Dearborn, Michigan; Leah Ruto, Casa Esperanza Montessori Dual-Language Preschool and Charter School, Raleigh, North Carolina

# PHOTO CREDITS

**Jacket:** © Chuck Fishman.

**Title Page:** © National Dance Institute of New Mexico. **Title Spread:** © Bob Schatz. Pages 4–5: © Heidi Jo Brady. **Contents:** page 6 top, © John Elk III/Lonely Planet Images; page 6 bottom and page 7, © Jeff Greenberg/The Image Works. **What is it like to be a child in the U.S.A.?:** page 8 top, © Jeff Greenberg/The Image Works; page 8 bottom, © Megan Carr; page 9 top, © The News Journal; page 9 bottom, left to right, © G.R. Lindblade and Co., © Tony Savino Photography, Inc./The Image Works, © Rommel Pecson/The Image Works; page 10 top, © Steve Linsenmeyer; page 10 bottom, © Johnny Sundby; page 11, © Lisa Berman.

**Montgomery, Alabama:** page 14 top, © Valerie Downes; page 14 bottom, © David Bundy/ Montgomery Advertiser; page 15 top, © Tammy McKinley/Montgomery Advertiser; page 15 bottom, © Valerie Downes/SPLC. **Barrow, Alaska:** page 16 top, © Fred Hirschmann; page 16 bottom, © Ken Graham/Accent Alaska.com; page 17 top and bottom, © Luciana Whitaker/Accent Alaska.com. **Tucson, Arizona:** page 18 top and bottom, © Stephen Trimble; page 19 top, © Matt Bradley/bciusa.com; page 19 bottom, © Michael B. Schwartz/Tucson Arts Brigade. **Little Rock, Arkansas:** page 20 top, Photo courtesy of the Little Rock Convention and Visitors Bureau; page 20 bottom and page 21 top, © Katherina-Marie Yancy/¡Hola! Arkansas; page 21 bottom, © Richard Lord Enterprises/The Image Works. **San Francisco, California:** page 22 top, © John Henry Williams/bciusa.com; page 22 bottom, © Champions Run for Children photo by Gene Cohn/RhodyCo Productions, used with permission; page 23 top, © Mark Downey; page 23 bottom, © Lawrence Migdale/Mira Images. **Denver, Colorado:** page 24, © Denver Post; page 25 top, © Kent Meireis/The Image Works; page 25 center, © Jack Olson; page 25 bottom, © Denver Metro Convention & Visitors Bureau. **New Haven, Connecticut:** page 26 top, © Vizion/The Image Works; page 26 bottom, © Wojtek Wacowski/ AMISTAD America, Inc.; page 27 top and bottom, © Michael Doolittle/The Image Works. **Wilmington, Delaware:** page 28 and page 29 , all photos, © The News Journal. **Washington, District of Columbia:** page 30 top, © Brent Winebrenner/Lonely Planet Images; page 30 bottom, © Joanne Pearson/Fair Haven Photographs; page 31 top, © Carol Pratt; page 31 bottom, © Gibson Stock Photography. **Miami, Florida:** page 32 top, © Jeff Greenberg/The Image Works; page 32 bottom, © Tony Savino Photography, Inc./The Image Works; page 33 top, © Kristin Gunnars; page 33 bottom, © Jeff Greenberg/ Photo Researchers. **Atlanta, Georgia:** page 34 and page 35, all photos, © Michael Schwarz Photography, Inc./The Image Works. **Honolulu, Hawaii:** page 36 top, © David Schrichte/ Photo Resource Hawaii; page 36 bottom, © John Elk III; page 37 top, © Heather Titus/ Photo Resource Hawaii; page 37 center, © Monte Costa/Photo Resource Hawaii; page 37 bottom, © Franco Salmoiraghi/ Photo Resource Hawaii. **Boise, Idaho:** page 38 top, © Chad Chase/Idaho Stock Images; page 38 bottom, © David Frazier/The Image Works; page 39 top, © William Mullins/ Idaho Stock Images; page 39 bottom, © Lee Foster/bciusa.com. **Chicago, Illinois:** page 40 top, © Chicago Convention and Tourism Bureau; page 40 bottom, © Paul Wasserman; page 41 top, © Heidi Jo Brady; page 41 bottom, © Russell Gordon. **Fort Wayne, Indiana:** page 42 top, © Cathie Rowand/ The Journal Gazette; page 42 bottom, © Andy Barrand; page 43 top, © Cheryl Ertelt/Photos and Phrases; page 43 bottom, © Michelle Lechlitner/Berne Chamber of Commerce. **Sioux City, Iowa:** page 44 top, © Dorothy Pecaut Nature Center; page 44 bottom and page 45 top and bottom, © G.R. Lindblade and Co. **Topeka, Kansas:** page 46 top, © Bill Stephens; page 46 bottom, © Shawn Malone; page 47 top, © Ben Weddle/MIDWESTOCK; page 47 bottom, © Mark Hood.

# PHOTO CREDITS

Pearson/Fair Haven Photographs; page 93 center, © Frank Siteman/Stone/Getty Images; page 93 bottom, © Sts. Sahag & Mesrob Armenian Apostolic Church. **Charleston, South Carolina:** page 94 and page 95, © Courtesy of Charleston County Parks and Recreation Commission. **Rapid City, South Dakota:** page 96 top and bottom, and page 97 top, © Johnny Sundby; page 97 center, © Kathryn Reeves; page 97 bottom, © John Elk III. **Nashville, Tennessee:** page 98 top and page 99 top, © Peyton Hoge; page 98 bottom, © Bounthanh Manivong/Royal Lao Classical Dancers; page 99 bottom, © Bob Schatz. **Houston, Texas:** page 100 top, © Ann Purcell; page 100 bottom, © Children's Museum of Houston; page 101 top, © 2006 Jim Olive/Stockyard.com; page 101 bottom, © Space Center Houston. **Salt Lake City, Utah:** page 102, © Richard Cheski; page 103 top and bottom, © Stephen Trimble; page 103 center, © Peggi Nash/Intermountain Therapy Animals. **Burlington, Vermont:** page 104 top, © Marybeth Redmond; page 104 bottom, © Mike Brinson/The Image Bank/Getty Images; page 105 top, © The Intervale Center; page 105 center, © Alden Pellett/The Image Works; page 105 bottom, © Richard Nowitz. **Richmond, Virginia:** page 106 and page 107, all photos, © Al Wekolo. **Seattle, Washington:** page 108 top, © Earl Harper/EcoStock; page 108 bottom, © Gibson Stock Photography; page 109 top, © Frozen Images/The Image Works; page 109 bottom, © Norbert Von Der Groeben/The Image Works. **Wheeling, West Virginia:** page 110 top, © Wheeling National Heritage Area Corporation; page 110 bottom, © PhotriMicroStock™/S. Shaluta, Jr.; page 111 top, © Steve Shaluta/WV Commerce; page 111 center, © Charlotte Khourey/Our Lady of Lebanon Church; page 111 bottom, © Wheeling Symphony Youth Orchestra. **Milwaukee, Wisconsin:** page 112 top, © German Fest Milwaukee, Inc.; page 112 bottom, © Lisa Berman; page 113 top, center, and bottom, © Susan L. Ruggles/Index Stock Imagery. **Cheyenne, Wyoming:** page 114 top, © Mary Steinbacher/Photonica/Getty Images; page 114 bottom, © Jon Asher; page 115 top, © Lori Hunter; page 115 bottom, © John & Yva Momatiuk/The Image Works.

**Resources:** page 116, © Debra L. Ferguson, Southern Images Photography; page 117, © City of Chicago; page 118 top left, © Al Wekolo; page 118 top right, © Albert Rizvanov; page 118 bottom left, © Sandra Stambaugh; page 118 bottom right, © Roland Dumuk; page 119, © The Center for Grieving Children. **Index:** page 120, © Trina Fimple; page 121, © Sandra Stambaugh; page 122, © Champions Run for Children photo by Gene Cohn/RhodyCo Productions, used with permission; page 123, © Susan Pfannmuller/MIDWESTOCK. **Acknowledgments:** page 124, © David Bundy/Montgomery Advertiser. **Photo Credits:** page 125, © Mario Tama/Reportage/Getty Images. page 126, © Ken Graham/Accent Alaska.com; page 127, © Michael Karas. **Dedications Page:** page 128, © Vizion/The Image Works.